105

GENESIS REGAINED

Genesis Regained

F. J. SHEED

"Go to the giant Genesis and the engendering of all things."
—*Piers Plowman*

Sheed and Ward · London and Sydney

First published 1969
Sheed and Ward Ltd, 33 Maiden Lane, London WC2, and
Sheed and Ward Pty Ltd, 204 Clarence Street, Sydney NSW 2000

© *F. J. Sheed* 1969

SBN 7220 0598 9

Made and printed in Great Britain by
Wood Westworth & Co. Ltd., St. Helens, Lancs.

Contents

Introduction

THOUGH GENESIS REGAINED is the title, this book is principally about Genesis' first three chapters. They are the root out of which Genesis grows. In them we find scriptural writing in the pure state. They are more discussed than all the rest of the Old Testament put together. And to them the word "regained" is the most aptly applied.

From whom had they to be regained?

Not so much from those who are violently for them or violently against them. The Tom Payne, Mark Twain sort of attack is as out-of-date as the Dayton Tennessee sort of fundamentalism. Right into this century, of course, it was mostly attack, and on two fronts—Evolution proved the Genesis stories of the world's beginnings and man's to be nonsense; and a study of Near Eastern mythology proved them to be of the same order, only fumigated and de-sexed.

Today the attack has faded, while the study has ramified in all directions. Those who gave themselves to it are unaligned, so to speak, or not violently aligned. It is they who have made Genesis so hard to find, the sheer mass of their scholarship has made it seem inaccessible. Its first three chap-

ters, which are my main concern, total only about fifteen
hundred words (more or fewer according to the language in
which one reads them). Only fifteen hundred words; but
microscopically studied, learnedly discussed, heatedly argued
about—no group throws up more heat than the pure scholars,
the unaligned. In action have been (among others) astron-
omers, geologists, biologists, geneticists; comparative religion-
ists, archaeologists, anthropologists, philologists; to say
nothing of Scripture scholars and theologians. In such clouds
of learning, Genesis itself got lost.

The clouds are clearing, mainly because even the negative-
destruction criticism has proved to be usable positively, for
construction. Augustine stated the principle that where facts
seem to contradict revelation, we must re-examine both.
Applying this, theologians and Scripture men have seen
meanings in Genesis which, but for the bothering facts,
would have remained hidden. Genesis has been, or is being,
found again.

Because the opening of Genesis treats of the creation by
God of man and the universe, its study calls for theology
(Judaeo-Christian and pagan), anthropology and the natural
sciences; to these, because of where we find Genesis, we must
add Scripture. No one can specialize in more than one of
these fields—my own labors have been in theology; of the
other fields one must learn from those who have labored in
them. This, to the best of my power, I have done.

With all the ramifying, the main questions about Genesis
1-3 still are their relation to the ancient myths and the new-
est sciences—especially to the possibility of a single first
couple and the improbability of a paradisal beginning. I
treat these, in the light of what scholarship tells us; but they
are not what I am writing about. I treat them only in so far
as they are obstacles to the clear seeing of the three chapters.
Again, I compare what they actually contain to the towering

structure of theology, Original Sin especially, built upon them. But this too is only for the clearer seeing of the chapters themselves—what the writers were saying to their own world, what they can say to ours—without this last it would be mere archaism to write about them.

When Chapters 2 and 3 were written, I was not there to observe—any more than their author observed man's creation by God. As to how the author set about writing the book and carried it through to completion, I can only guess —so must any other critic; and as to what was in his mind at point after point of the writing, I can only guess. But my guessing is not wholly in the dark. As a publisher I have had forty years of close contact with scores of authors in the actual process of writing—from the first idea, through every sort of anguish, to the finished manuscript. One develops an intuition about the writing mind at work; rather like the intuition a sailor has of sea or sky, though less likely to be right, I fear. It is this intuition which has guided such guessing as I have had to do.

GENESIS REGAINED

1

Why Genesis?

I

GENESIS, A GREEK WORD for "beginning," is the first of five
books (that is what the Greek word Pentateuch means)
which tell of beginnings—the beginning of the universe, of
man, of the Jewish people and its choice by God as especially
his own. The Pentateuch begins with the earth formless and
void and ends with Moses dying and the Israelites on the
verge of the Promised Land.

It was revered by the Jews, and in due course by Christians,
as Torah, the Law, coming from the hand of Moses himself
round 1200 B.C. In the first excitements of modern linguistic
and archaeological discoveries, Moses as author became matter for derision—it was said, for instance, that writing was
not known in Palestine in his day (actually there was more
than one alphabet), that he could not have written the description of his own death at the end of Deuteronomy, that
Leviticus treats of a highly developed liturgical and cere-
monial religion unthinkable in the desert and assumes a
religio-political structure which reached its high point with
David and Solomon two or three hundred years after Moses.

3

Besides all this the Pentateuch contains inconsistencies, contradictions, repetitions un-dovetailed, grammatical and literary forms certainly not of one period—all comprehensible if many writers were involved over many periods.

As it happens, the Pentateuch makes no claim to have Moses for author. The phrase which misled earlier readers was "Moses wrote this torah" (Deut. 31.9). But the Pentateuch does not call itself the Torah—that name for it came later. "Torah" was a normal word for any piece of teaching or moral instruction or legislation: the phrase just quoted is taken by most as referring only to the passage immediately before it or perhaps the one that follows.

For the rest, we find the Pentateuch referred to in the Old Testament as the book of the Law—of Yahweh or of Moses —or simply as the Law. What of the New? We find precisely those same phrases (Luke 24.44; Rom. 3.21; Gal. 3.10). But the special passage is in John 5. Christ has shown how the Baptist has borne testimony of him; so has the Father "by the works he has granted me to accomplish"; in any event "if you believed Moses, you would believe me, for he wrote of me." This is not a statement that Moses wrote the five books but that his writing is to be found in them: which is very much how Christ treated "Moses and all the prophets" when he showed the two disciples on the road to Emmaus "in all the Scriptures the things concerning himself" (Luke 24.27).[1]

Much in the five books was written after Moses' time: but he dominated the period of its beginnings and the whole thing is a genuine growth upon a tree genuinely his. So that Professor Albright can summarize the position: "It would be sheer hyper-criticism to deny the substantially Mosaic character of the Pentateuchal tradition."[2] All of which is very much what the Biblical Commission told Cardinal Suhard in 1948. "We invite Catholic scholars to study these problems

with an open mind in the light of sound criticism and of
the results of other sciences which have their part in these
matters, and such study will without doubt establish *the large
share and the profound influence* of Moses as author and as
legislator"—the words italicized by me being wider, at any
rate clearer, than the Commission's earlier "substantial au-
thenticity and Mosaic integrity of the Pentateuch."

Genesis is usually thought of as divisible into two—the
first eleven chapters are pre-history: with the appearance of
Abram, who was to be Abraham, we have moved into the
stream of history (somewhere between 1900 and 1750, hazards
Albright), and the remainder of the book is of him and the
Patriarchs descended from him. It ends with the death of
Joseph. The second book, Exodus, is all of Moses and the
movement of the Israelites out of Egypt and into the
desert.

But the first eleven chapters themselves are further divisible. They fall into three parts. Chapter 1 has the Creation
of the Universe, Chapters 2 and 3 tell of Adam and Eve and
the Fall. Chapters 4-11 tell, in a series of stories, of the moral
and social chaos ushered in by the Fall. My main concern is
with the first three chapters. The first, on the week of Creation, was written last. Scholars seem agreed in dating it at or
near the end of the Babylonian Captivity, round 500 B.C.
About this time it is thought that Genesis as we now have it
was compiled: this Prologue Chapter, beginning like the
Prologue to John's Gospel with "In the beginning," was seen
as necessary to set the Pentateuch in a wider frame. It may
have been written by one of the Compilers. Chapters 2 and 3,
and indeed most of the remainder of Genesis, had been
written three or four centuries earlier, possibly under King
Solomon, who seems to have made learning his special
"thing."

The Compilers had for their use three main bodies of written material called for convenience E, J, and P—the Elohist in which the word for God is Elohim; the Yahwist in which the word is Yahweh (the German scholars spell it Jahweh because the German alphabet has no Y); the Priestly, which provides most of the liturgical and ritual and legislative sections of the Pentateuch. In our study of the first three chapters it is P and J that we meet. The first chapter is Priestly, with God as Elohim. Chapters 2 and 3 are Yahwist, with God as Yahweh-Elohim (J sometimes uses Elohim, but only he uses Yahweh). The Elohist comes in with Abraham. Whole libraries have been written on them and on D (for Deuteronomist). I give here the view which seems to be generally accepted as of the present moment. But there are differences among scholars—Father de Vaux of the Ecole Biblique, for instance, prefers to speak of an Elohistic Tradition rather than of a Document E.

The generally accepted view is that J came out of the Southern Kingdom, Judah, between 925 and 750, E out of the Northern, Israel, somewhat later. J and E, which cover roughly the same history, had already been brought together before P got to work on them—probably after the destruction of the Northern Kingdom in 722, possibly during the reign of the admirable Josias.

As first seen by Wellhausen and his followers, J, E and P were treated too much as sources rather than termini, with Moses dismissed as author, and the Biblical Commission reacting vigorously. But termini they were. Behind both Yahwist and Elohist there may well have been other documents; there certainly was a long tradition going back to Moses and further back still into Egypt and Mesopotamia. In *Peake's Commentary*, S. H. Hooke points out that "many of the laws and institutions had extra-Biblical parallels (Mesopotamian,

Assyrian, Hittite) much earlier than the dates attributed to the documents, and many of the narratives evidently arose in a milieu other and older." J and E, thinks Professor Albright, are both based on an epic narrative recited in Egypt before the Exodus: he finds the Genesis stories "swarming with poetic phraseology" and "strewn with reminiscences of the original verse form."[3]

However this may be, a strong argument not only for a tradition but for an authoritative tradition, behind J and E is drawn from the contradictions left unreconciled in the final compilation. The compilers were quite capable of seeing, for example, the difference between the one pair of each living thing taken into the Ark (Gen. 6.19-20 and 7.15) and the seven pairs of clean and one of unclean mentioned in 7.2; and between forty days and nights of rain (7.4,12) and a hundred and fifty days (7.24). It is argued that they felt it out of their power to attempt any reconciling or dovetailing. Both Flood stories had come to them with authority: they simply gave them both.

Who were the compilers? In the *Anchor Bible* edition of Genesis, the Jewish scholar E. A. Speiser gives his opinion that there had been a continuing supervision of tradition, written and spoken, by a priestly "school" of writers, and that by this school the P sections were written and the final compilation of J, E and P were made at the end of the Babylonian Captivity round 500 B.C.

There is general agreement that, unlike J and E, P was not one continuous document—scholars have traced up to ten P documents! They are better seen, perhaps, as insertions into the (primarily narrative) J and E "stream." P's interests are, as one might expect, official and impersonal—liturgy, ritual and legislation (practically the whole of Leviticus belongs to P, the end of Exodus and a good deal of Numbers):

the occasional narratives have an official emphasis. Again as one might expect, there is concern to establish Israel's special relation with God and its unbroken connection with the beginnings of things, especially the new beginning with Noah: the writers revel in genealogies. They would have been desolated by the von Rad theory that the history from Abraham to the death of Moses was a late invention, as they would by the assertion, confidently made (not by von Rad!) that Abraham was a heathen fertility God. But, our present concern is only with the first three Chapters of Genesis: our withers are unwrung. Our acceptance is grounded deeper.

Many sources have flowed into our Genesis. But whatever the origin of the materials they used, the first chapter was written by one man, so were Chapters 2-3. A story as closely knit as that of Adam and the Fall—its details selected so carefully and fitted so skilfully, nothing by chance—does not emerge from a people's consciousness; someone wrote it. And before I had read Dr. Speiser I had already made my own his view that the man who wrote Chapters 2-3 (and most of the eight chapters which follow) was one of the world's great writers. Gerhard von Rad agrees with the view that the artistic mastery in his narrative is one of the greatest accomplishments of all times in the history of thought. Nor was anything as patterned as the Hymn of Creation in Chapter 1 produced by a people's religious mind and experience, though all its elements may have been: someone constructed it. For convenience, I shall refer to them as the Priest and the Yahwist.

II

So the Genesis story is satisfactorily old. But what authority has it? Why should we take it as anything more than an early effort to account for man's presence on the earth—a great advance on myths earlier still, but of no more authority than the reader feels moved to concede to some of its insights? What could Moses in the thirteenth century, or the compiler in the sixth, know of the beginnings of the human race thirty thousand years, or three hundred thousand years, before?

Until the geological and archaeological revelations and revolutions of the last hundred years, the historical reliability of Genesis was guaranteed to the unhistorically-minded, always a majority, by the ages of the Patriarchs. The lives of three men—Adam, Methuselah, Noah—spanned the centuries between creation and Abraham. Abraham was sixty when Noah died and must have had many a talk with him! Abraham told Isaac, Isaac told Jacob; the space between Jacob and Moses presented no problem, given the genealogical passion of men then and their marvellous memories. So great a thinker as Pascal could write in the *Pensées*, "Sem, who saw Lamech who saw Adam, at least saw Abraham, who saw Jacob, who saw those who beheld Moses; therefore the Flood and the Creation are true."

But the writer or writers of the first eleven chapters did not know about the evidence fossils would some day yield of vast geological ages, or the evidence the archaeologists would find of forgotten civilizations and of human remains behind the civilizations. He knew only that creation had happened a long time ago. The Sumerians had listed nine kings before the Flood and ten after; so in his chapter he did likewise, save that he listed ten on each side of the Flood, and his men were patriarchs not kings. In accord with his view that everything earlier was far away in an immeasurable past, he gave immense ages to the patriarchs he named—though not as immense as the Sumerians gave: Methuselah's 969 years was a flash compared with the 65,000 of Sumeria's oldest.

We may doubt if he thought Methuselah really lived as

long as that, or thought much about it at all. Any more than
he would have bothered to work out (as one scholar does)
that when Jacob's mother sent him back to Canaan for fear
the local girls would entrap him into marriage, he must have
been rising seventy. Old men, of course, can make fools of
themselves with women; but one feels Jacob's youthfulness,
especially in his wooing and winning of Rachel—he would
have been well up in the eighties when at last he married her.

Numbers had not the same bearing in that world as in
ours. For us they represent a way of counting, they belong to
arithmetic. In those distant days arithmetic was pretty ele-
mentary (compared with geometry, for instance). Numbers
belonged to rhetoric and symbolism. "Saul has slain his
thousands and David his tens of thousands" (1 Sam. 18.7)
was a perfectly normal way of saying that the victory had
been won by David not Saul, because David had slain Go-
liath. One theory is that the Yahwist knew that the beginning
was a long time before Abraham, and only ten names had
come down to him, so he gave them a vast number of years
each. Another is that the vast ages given to the patriarchs
symbolized their greatness, which in both lists diminished as
they got further from the beginning. We cannot be sure of
the original Genesis writer's ranking of the patriarchs because
the ages differ in the Hebrew Bible, the Greek translation
made by the Jews of Alexandria, and the Samaritan books of
Moses. But in general we note that before the Flood the ages
run between 900 plus and 700, from the Flood to Abraham
between 600 and 200, from Abraham on between 200 and
100. The exception among the pre-Flood men was number 7,
Enoch, who is given only 365 years, after which "he was not,
for God took him." Sumeria's number 7 had been "taken up
to the gods to hear secrets not divulged to men."

For the orthodox Jew and for the Christian, the authority

of the Creation story comes from its being Scripture, the inspired word of God. For the Christian there is something more. Christ made it his own by quoting Genesis 2.24—"Therefore a man leaves his father and mother and cleaves to his wife, and they become one flesh." Indeed he gives it greater authority than it gives itself. For, merely reading the passage, we would assume that we are to take the words as spoken by the writer, or possibly by Adam. But Christ says that God said them (Matt. 19.4-5)—"He who made them from the beginning made them male and female *and said. . . .*"

Inspiration is discussed at length in Chapter 5 of my *God and the Human Mind.* Some points are worth noting here, especially this—that inspiration is not one undifferentiated process. In essence it means that the writers wrote what God wanted written. But they are not machines, not even stenographers. With mind illumined and will guided by God, each is yet writing as himself, writing what he wants to write. God's action in mind and will could not be the same—existentially—on John writing in his Gospel of the situation at the creation of the world and before it, and of events he had himself witnessed; on Paul writing his letter to the Romans in all its doctrinal profundity and the same Paul writing to Philemon about a runaway slave; on the men (whoever they were) who wrote the book of Genesis seven or eight hundred years after the last of the events it records, and on Luke writing the Acts of the Apostles thirty years or so after the first of its happenings.

What I have called the existential variation in the inspiring of Scripture had already been sensed by the Jews. They thought the first five books wholly inspired, the writings of the Prophets less wholly so, the rest written by men vari-

ously aided by God. And for the Christians the coming of
Christ made Revelation new as it made all things new: and
in its newness Revelation made Inspiration new, just as it
gave teaching authority the newness of infallibility.

How God influenced the writer while leaving him free is
his own secret. One fact about it we can see—the writer need
not know that God is inspiring him, as the writer of the
Apocalypse did: he may be writing down his own thought
with guidance from God of which he has no suspicion. Thus
Second Macchabees is the summarization of a five-volume
work by Jason of Cyrene, and the man who wrote the summary tells us what a sweating labor it was. We have all
experienced something sufficiently like this in our response
to actual grace; we think a particular matter out for ourselves and arrive at decisions in light which is in fact given
us by God, ourselves never suspecting the source of the light
in which we have come to see the situation.

But even if we feel that a given man might have written
exactly the same book without inspiration from God, the
fact that God has been in action makes the book a different
reality, as water with the Holy Spirit is a different reality
from plain water, though no chemical test would show the
difference. The Holy Spirit *abides* in Scripture; reading it
we can make contact with him to the limit of our willing-
ness.

Does everything in an inspired book come to us with the
authority of the God who cannot deceive? Certainly there
are things in these books which are simply not so, things
which contradict each other. Yet God wanted them written.
He submitted himself to human limitations, man's ignorance
in particular, where this submission did not cut across his
own purpose. But what was his purpose in wanting these
books written? For many of them, or for sections in them,

the answer may be that he wanted them written because he
wanted them recorded, that is preserved; and he wanted
them preserved that we might all be able to follow the movement of mankind on its way to Christ: these are the stages
through which men passed, the ideas men had as their minds
grew towards the fullness of revelation.

Genesis is a compilation. The compiler (there may have
been more than one) put in Chapter 1 and the much earlier
Chapters 2-3 as he found them, not trying to dovetail them
—they had come to him with authority, and he assumed no
right to alter them. How far, in the form in which we now
have them, is each the work of a single author? And in what
sense are they of divine inspiration? Were the writers inspired to write them, or only the compiler to include them?
I have given my reason for thinking each the work of a single
man. How did the one arrive at the Hymn of Creation, the
other at the story of Eden?

The idea of a revelation given to the first man and preserved through the centuries seemed less improbable when
there were thought to be only thirty of these centuries. What
of a revelation given by God to Moses? Maybe. But it does
not seem probable: the revelation actually given him—of
the choosing of Israel by God as especially his people, of the
covenant, of the promises—was already vast. It is idle to pretend that we know. But a man of profound religious insight
meditating on the "I am" of Exodus 3, guided in his meditation not only by centuries of priestly concentration on it
but by actual graces of whose action he need have known
nothing, might have produced the Hymn of Creation. And
an earlier man of the same sort, similarly aided, concentrating all the power of his mind on the gulf between what
God wanted and the world which actually is, might have
produced the story of Eden and the Fall.

NOTES

1. *The Revised Standard Version and the Apocrypha,* copyrighted 1957 by the Division of Christian Education, National Council of the Churches of Christ in the U.S.A., and used by permission. Unless another version is indicated or the translation is literal, all Scripture quotations in this book are from the *Revised Standard Version.*

2. W. F. Albright, *The Bible and the Ancient Near East* (New York, Doubleday, 1961).

3. *Ibid.*

2

Myths of Creation

AT EVERY POINT in our discussion of the first three chapters of Genesis, the myths the writers must have known—Egyptian, Mesopotamian, Canaanite—will be considered. The purpose is twofold:

To see what the myths made of the problems presented by the existence of the universe;

To see what the Genesis men made of the myths.

For success, it is not sufficient that we make skeleton summaries of each, then compare and contrast the skeletons. It is not easy to get inside either, where the life is. But the deeper we penetrate into Genesis and myths as they were lived, the surer will our judgment be. Elements which look identical in the skeletons often look quite different in the living fact. What I try to give here is a beginning of penetration. It can be only a beginning. I have listed some books which will help the reader to continue his study in depth.

I

There was Egypt where the Jews had been for an uncertain number of centuries till Moses, born and reared there and bearing an Egyptian name, brought them out; and where they were to return in such numbers that Alexandria would become a capital of world Jewry and Elephantine, in the Nile, have a Temple which maintained correspondence with the Temple in Jerusalem.

We can trace the myths back a couple of thousand years before the arrival in Egypt of the Israelites; and even as early as 3000 B.C., when Lower and Upper Egypt first became one, they were bewildering in their variety. Discoveries continually being made render it difficult to speak with the confidence of fifty years ago. But the main outlines seem fairly clear.

There were two main systems. (1) The sky gods, Re and the rest, who provide the creation stories, seem to have come from Asia: according to the sophistication of the worshipper, Re was either the sun, or a god who made the sun his chariot, or a god of whom the sun was the apt symbol. (2) The vegetation gods—dying and rising again with the seasons—may also have come from the East: there was an Osiris cult in Syria: but Petrie thinks that the Libyans to the west were worshipping Osiris earlier still.

I have called them "systems," but there was no real system in either, only shifting patterns; no dogmas, nothing to prevent interweavings and identifications, nothing to hinder linking Re and Osiris with each other, or with the animal cults which antedated both, and which for the mass of Egyptians may have been religion's daily bread! Osiris was imaged as a bull or a hawk, Hathor as a cow. Reading the myths in both major series, we note how profoundly they were conditioned by the Nile, on whose flowing all Egypt's prosperity depended, whose flooding could threaten all.

Since our concern is with creation, the genesis of the cosmos, we concentrate on the Re series. The universe did not begin with Re. It began with a watery chaos, as did the

Sumerian, but with touches special to the Nile. The word for the original chaos was Nun, later to be clothed with personality and divinity. First came Atum; from Atum came Shu, the god of the atmosphere, and his consort Tefnut. In Hermopolis, between Atum and these two, they inserted eight divine beings, the Ogdoad—four couples (the males with frogs' heads, the females with serpents'); the fourth couple were Amun, the air, and his lady: Amun was to rise very high in the pantheon.

Sex was the one creative force the Egyptians saw as primary, the principle of all. Once Shu and Tefnut had come to exist there was no problem—they produced Geb, the earth, and Nut, the sky, in the natural way of sex; and the rest of the gods followed naturally. But when there was only Atum, how did he produce Shu and Tefnut? He spat out the one and vomited the other, said one account. But the legend which had him bring them into being by masturbating—he "took his phallus in his hand to stimulate desire" —seems more in the spirit of that age and place.

To a people so single-minded, as to early peoples generally (but not to the Old Testament writers), Sky and Earth—the one stretched over the other, with the fertilizing fluid falling from one to the other—could not fail to suggest the sex act. Baal, the Canaanite storm God, dwelling in the sky, was called "the spouse of the fields." We are told that the Hindu bridegroom says to the bride, "I am the sky, you are the earth." Examples are everywhere. A curiosity with the Egyptians was that Geb, the earth, was male and Nut, the sky, was female, so that in an ancient Egyptian love song the man says, "I am the earth." This may have been a way of representing the simple fact that whereas in most countries the earth is fertilized by rain from above, in Egypt all fertility came from the Nile at earth level. Or it may be that this was the Egyptian mating posture. Or again it may have been

mere grammatical chance, earth and sky already having their
genders before the myth gave them sex.

Whatever the reason, it suited those of the Sun God's
worshippers who believed him born in the womb of the Sky
—necessarily, therefore, female. Another curiosity is that
among the gods origin did not constitute primacy. Re, who
came after Earth and Sky, was seen as mightier than the gods
who came before him and the gods who came after.

In the course of the millennia the myth knew variations.
There were variations within the series. It was expressed in
a ritual, and the ritual could blossom into other myths. Further, as domination passed from one town to another,
Heliopolis, Memphis, Hermopolis, Thebes—the town of the
moment had to see itself as the first to rise above the surface
of Nun, and its god must be given a special part in the creative process. Memphis had Ptah, "the Opener," a Semitic
name. Thebes had Amun, "the Hidden One," seventh in the
Ogdoad: he had risen from obscurity as local god of Karnak
round 2200, was adopted as their own by the Pharaohs of
the Twelfth Dynasty, and with Thebes as his center came
to be called King of the Gods.

There were intermarriages, so to speak, between series. In
Heliopolis, a thousand years before Abraham, Geb and Nut
of the sky series were shown as the parents of Osiris, one of
the vegetation series, and so of his sister and wife Isis, and
of his brother Set, god of the desert. Osiris and Isis had a
son Horus who over the centuries became the key figure in
the series, ruler of the sky, the falcon his symbol. In one
version he became Osiris after Osiris had been slain by Set.
At one point a second Horus emerged. And in the fourteenth
century Rameses II gave supremacy to Set.

While the Israelites were in Egypt, a century or so before
the Exodus, the Pharaoh Amenhotep IV had made a move
in the direction of monotheism. He proclaimed one deity—

Aton, the sun's disk—changed his own name to Akhenaton, and made a determined effort to stamp out the worship of all others, that of Amun of Thebes especially. For the first time there was official religious persecution among the Egyptians—in the interests of monotheism! His reign was short, and the effort failed. But actually the theologians had always been feeling towards a single God. In the centuries after 3000 B.C. the kings had been deified—Re having managed to visit their mothers intimately: that was the period of the Pyramids, the concentration of all interest upon the Pharaoh's life after death. (At the very beginning a Pharaoh's leading courtiers may have been buried with him.) By the middle of that millennium all this had passed: there was still the concentration on life after death, but not for kings only. The kings were men not gods—at least for the better-educated: their deity lasted among the mass of people till long after Moses had led the Israelites out of Egypt.

The tendency to merge the high gods had grown: Re-Atum, Horus-Re, Amun-Re—"Amun, he who conceals his name, is Re as to his face, Ptah as to his body." What this meant to their worshippers we cannot know with any certainty. One who himself practises a religion is better equipped to understand another who practises a religion—any religion, even one which strikes him as intellectually incredible or morally repulsive. He knows what movements of mind or heart are in action. In the matter of the Egyptian myths, he has an advantage over one, perhaps more learned, in whom those movements are dormant or twisted against themselves. But the best-equipped Egyptologist, practising a religion, cannot *be* an ancient Egyptian. There is too much which he—and we—can but surmise. To us it would seem sheerly comic, for instance, that the animal god of pregnant women should have been the hippopotamus, with the abiding pregnancy of its shape. But the idea met some profound need in Egyptian

women through two or three thousand years: they would
have a figure of the hippopotamus in their house. It has been
suggested that the women had the consolation of knowing
that within a few months they would return to a better shape
while the hippopotamus must continue to look pregnant: but
this belongs to our age not theirs.

It would seem that there was no automatic rivalry among
the worshippers of different gods. We may take an extreme
case. Across the river from Heliopolis, center of the Nun-
Atum-Re series, lay Memphis, which very early proclaimed
its own Ptah as prior to, or creator of, Atum. In *Mythologies
of the Ancient World,* S. N. Kramer expresses the view that
this was not necessarily meant as polemic against Heliopolis
—"There is no evidence that mythological concepts were
employed as political chessmen by belligerent theologians."[1]

Our concern, we remind ourselves, is with creation, the
beginning, what has come to be called Protology. We have
seen that Atum first emerged from the waste of water, and
produced Shu and Tefnut. As to what lay between these two
and the whole pantheon, the myths proliferated. There could
hardly have been an Egyptian who knew them all. Consider
three of the most important of those which treat of the "how"
of creation—in Hermopolis, in Thebes, in Memphis.

With Hermopolis we have the cosmic egg which contained
Re, who was to be creator of all things human and divine.
Our own immediate irreverent question would be "Who
laid the cosmic egg?" It would not have troubled the worshippers of Re, save as irreverence: they would have responded better, perhaps, to Freud's idea that it meant a wish
to return to the womb! The full notion of eternity, as abiding
present with no beginning and no end, no before and no
after, had not reached them. They assumed that there must
have been a beginning; and they were prepared for an end,

the gods too might die. But instinctively, one imagines, they knew that the beginning was mysterious. They did not expect answers which would account for everything. They tested the myth, not by its external demonstrability or even its inner logic, but by its livability. It was sufficient that they felt their life richer because of it.

For Thebes, Amun, with no father or mother, laid his own egg. "All other gods came into being when he himself made the beginning of being. He abides in heaven as Re." The ancient Egyptian then, like the modern astronomer, was content to start with a first being actually there, not asking why it, or anything, should have existed at all. One way or another, everything else was the unfolding of all the possibilities wrapped up in the first being—Atum discharging his semen, or the first atom exploding, into the universe we know.

This process of "dismemberment" reached a high point with the third of Egypt's creation myths—that of Ptah, related in the Memphis *Theology of Creation,* a straight narrative with dialogues inserted. As we have it, scholars place it round 700 B.C. but hold that it comes from two thousand years earlier. Ptah the primeval ocean, both male and female, was father and mother of Atum whom he absorbed into himself—"There came into being as the heart, and there came into being as the tongue, something in the form of Atum. The mighty great one is Ptah"—in other words, Ptah thought of Atum, and spoke him into existence. "The mighty great one is Ptah who transmitted life to all gods through his heart by which Horus became Ptah, through the tongue by which Thoth became Ptah. Through heart and tongue, thought and utterance, Ptah is in every body and in the mouth of all gods, all men, all cattle, all creeping things and all that lives." His teeth and lips did what Atum's semen and hands did to produce the Ennead—the Nine, made up of Ogdoad plus Ptah himself—"which pronounced the name

of everything, from which Shu and Tefnut came forth." The
concluding words are "And so Ptah was satisfied,"[2] which one
may according to taste interpret as "Ptah rested" or "Ptah
saw that it was good."

The Egyptians were prepared, we have noted, for an end.
In the *Book of the Dead* Atum says to Osiris:

> *In the end I will destroy everything that I
> have created.*
> *The earth will become again part of the pri-
> meval ocean*
> *Like the Abyss of waters in their original
> state.*
> *Then I will be what will remain, just I and
> Osiris.*
> *When I will have changed myself back into
> the Old Serpent*
> *Who knew no man and saw no god.*[3]

The Egyptian creation myths are almost entirely of gods.
There is a papyrus of round 1300 B.C. which has "Then men
came into being," with no word of "how." There is a fif-
teenth-century hymn to Amun—"Thou from whose eyes
came men, and from whose mouth sprang the gods." This is
scarcely more illuminating. Nor is the legend of a lotus transformed into a boy, from whose tears the first men were
formed. The creation of men clearly struck myth-makers as
a minor matter, beneath their dignity perhaps. Not so their
opposite numbers in Mesopotamia.

II

The Mesopotamian influence is more clearly visible in the
Old Testament than the Egyptian. There are similarities of

detail—in the order of creation, in the stories of the Fall and the Flood, in the Patriarchs and their vast ages; and the Tower of Babel is, of course, Babylonian. Israel's roots were in Mesopotamia. It was from Haran, close on four thousand years ago, that Abraham began the great wandering which has not yet ended. Joshua could say to the leaders of Israel: "Thus says the Lord God: 'Your fathers lived of old beyond the Euphrates—Terah, the father of Abraham and of Nahor; and they served other gods' " (Jos. 24.2). Who were these gods and how were they served?

We begin with the Sumerians, a non-Semitic people, who moved into what we now think of as Babylonia (Scripture calls it Senanar) round the year 4000 B.C. By 3000, about the time of the first union of Higher and Lower Egypt, their civilization was at its height, religiously and materially, with the great temple cities of Erech (or Uruk) and Nippur, to be joined, four hundred years later, by Ur. Round 2400, Sargon of Semitic Accad conquered Sumeria and established the world's first empire. With Hammurabi, round 1800, Babylon became the Great City. The Sumerians had disappeared, absorbed into their Accadian conquerors; but these largely adopted the Sumerian religion and liturgy, and Sumerian remained the liturgical language and the learned tongue of Western Asia (much as Latin would survive the end of the Roman Empire); a thousand years after Sargon's triumph, Sumerian was being studied in the schools of Syria and Asia Minor as well as of Mesopotamia and Susiana.[4]

But the rise of Babylon made one change inevitable. Its god Marduk was not in the Sumerian pantheon, already sufficiently multitudinous—three or four thousand divinities, with Nun enthroned at Erech, Enlil Lord of the Sky at Nippur. As Babylon came to tower over the other cities, Marduk, now described as Nun's grandson and later identified with Enlil, had to tower over the other gods. How this came to

B

be is told in a vast poem written during the first Babylonian dynasty (1894-1595), possibly during the reign of Hammurabi. From its opening words it is known as *Enuma elish,* "when on high":

> *When on high the heavens had not been named*
> *Firm ground below had not been called by name*
> *Naught but primordial Apsu, their begetter*
> *(And) Mummu-Tiamat, she who bore them all*
> *Their waters commingling as a single body*
> *When no gods whatever had been called into being . . .*
> *Then it was that the gods were formed within them.*[5]

Its special interest for us is in its account of creation. Already for the Sumerians there was a primordial chaos, Nammu; there were two rivers—Abzu (masculine) of fresh water, Tiamat (feminine) of salt. From Nammu came Enki, the god of water, and from him a host of other gods—Enlil, for example, who raped the child goddess Ninlil and so became father of Sin, the moon god.

In the *Enuma elish,* the rivers Apzu (now Apsu) and Tiamat are persons, divine persons. They had offspring, their grandson Anu had a son Enki, who became supreme, high above his ancestor gods and the gods his brothers.

Tiamat and Apsu began to resent the ways and manners of the young gods descended from them—the generation gap is to be found in most mythologies. Enki puts Apsu to sleep and slays him. Tiamat decides to avenge her husband. She produces a brood of monsters (of the Leviathan and Behemoth sort, only more so) and terrifies the gods with them. Even Enki, by the Babylonians called Ea, is afraid of Tiamat. But not Babylon's Marduk. He undertakes to go to war against her, on condition that he is to be Supreme God.

He kills Tiamat, though not without a struggle. He "splits her like a shell fish"; of one half of her body he makes the sky, of the other half the earth.

> With his unsparing mace he smashed her
>   skull.
> In her belly he established the zenith.[6]

And the gods say to Marduk, "We have granted thee kingship over the entire universe."

So Marduk reigned, at least in Babylonia; the temple tower they built for him—the "house of the Foundation Platform of Heaven and Earth"—may have suggested Scripture's Tower of Babel. It was destroyed by the Hittites, and Babylon itself conquered, round 1600, roughly when Jacob and his sons would have been moving into Egypt. But the worship of Marduk continued, and a thousand years later Babylon was once more enthroned above the nations with the Jewish people in captivity there. Six hundred years later, Apocalypse, the last book of the New Testament, still chooses Babylon as the name for the world empire arrayed against God.

From the time of its composition the *Enuma elish* continued to be recited annually in Marduk's temple during the first twelve days of the New Year. (Might Abraham's father have taken part? Might Abraham too? We are not certain enough of dates to be able to answer with confidence.) Marduk's fight against Tiamat was acted out by two groups, and his marriage with the goddess Sarpanitum re-enacted to the last detail in her sanctuary—a temple handmaid acting the

goddess's part. Mircea Eliade, who tells of this, thinks it
would have been followed by a general orgy.[7]

The Mesopotamian myths paid more attention than the
Egyptian to the making of man. The fullest story is in the
Enuma elish. Marduk said:

> *"Blood will I mass and cause bones to be.*
> *I will establish a savage, man shall be his*
> *   name."*[8]

But his father Enki (Ea) suggested a more interesting plan
—that one of the gods who had sided with Tiamat should
be slain and man made of his blood. And so it was done,
Kingu being chosen. There were variations. Some of these
were written, one feels, for the fun of it—the first efforts to
produce men, for instance, were failures, the gods being
drunk at the time. But most were serious.

In one, Marduk with Aruru, who was to be Earth Mother
as Ninhursag, created mankind, then animals, then the rivers
Tigris and Euphrates, vegetation . . . in another, the Sumerian god Anu created the heavens and Enki the earth,
Enki creating also lesser gods and men to use the earth for
the service of the first gods. Nor was this service always purely
religious. In another myth the gods find it difficult to get
their daily bread and men are made in order to do the work.
How are they made? "Mix their heart from the clay that is
over the abyss. . . . Bring their limbs into existence." Men's
raison d'être is stated again and again with clarity: the gods
needed them. In a late story two gods were slain, craftsmen
gods: of their blood men were made—to carry out the service
of the gods for all time.

The *Enuma elish* was Babylonian, though it used Sumerian mythology. The best-known Sumerian poem was the
Epic of Gilgamesh: we shall be looking at it in connection

with Adam and the Fall. Like the other Sumerian myths it
has nothing to give us about creation.

Neither have the myths of Canaan. These had more obvious effect than those of Egypt or Mesopotamia upon religion
as it was lived from day to day by the Israelites. Naturally,
for the Jews had conquered and occupied a great part of
Canaan; between the conquest under Joshua and the writing
of Genesis 2 and 3, the two nations had intermingled and
intermarried for as long a time as England has ceased to be
Catholic and America Indian. There was bound to be a
certain amount of religious infiltration. Some of it was natural and harmless. We are told, for instance, that the Jewish
Feast of Tabernacles was on the same day as a Canaanite
vintage festival—very much, one imagines, as our own Christmas Day has made its own the pagan festival day of Sol
Invictus. But there was too much of Canaanite religion
against which Jewish legislators and prophets had to rage.
There was the hurling of babies into the flames in honor of
Moloch. There were sodomy and bestiality—"By all these the
nations I am casting out before you defiled themselves; and
the land became defiled . . . the land vomited out its inhabit-
ants" (Lev. 18.24).

The high god of Canaan was El. And the word Elohim,
adopted by the Jews as their generic (so to speak) term for
God, was Canaanite. So was El Elyon, "God Most High,"
used of God by Abraham (Gen. 14.22). So was El Shaddai,
"God Almighty" or God of the mountain, the name by which
we read that God called himself when making covenant
with Abraham (Gen. 17.1).

Like Enki of the Sumerians, El yielded supremacy to the
most dynamic of the younger gods, Baal, the storm god. The
Canaanite pantheon was sufficiently like the Sumerian-
Babylonian. But where the religion of Mesopotamia was

concentrated on the order of the universe, with the Creation
Epic recited annually and other interests real but secondary,
the almost exclusive interest of Canaan was fertility. Baal,
god of storm, had become god of the crops!—"Spouse of the
Fields." The Baal-Anath cult was aimed at securing seven
years of good harvests. In all the paganisms the rituals were
necessary to the functioning of the universe—if they were
not performed, nature would not, could not, co-operate.

Because of the centering of religion upon fertility, the sex
act was at the liturgical center. The shrines of Baal, and of
fertility goddesses like Anath and Astarte, had prostitutes
male and female for the service of worshippers. And in the
springtime were the collective orgies, anyone with anyone,
incest alone barred.

Rebekah's reason for sending Jacob back from Canaan to
Mesoptotamia was that he might find a wife (Gen. 27.46).
If what she wanted for him was a wife free of Canaanite
abominations, it is ironical that when the Israelites left Egypt
it was to Canaan that God sent them as their promised land.
At any rate one can see why the Old Testament writers
thought that Canaan was only safe for the followers of Yahweh if the native population was literally exterminated: they
assumed that Yahweh would want them exterminated, and
therefore they said that this was his will.

The Canaanites were not exterminated of course. And
their religious practices proved only too alluring—bodily
union is sufficiently so in its own right; when proposed as a
religious duty it is just about irresistible.

Solomon built shrines "for Chemosh the abomination of
Moab, and for Molech the abomination of the Ammonites.
. . . And so he did for all his foreign wives" (1 Kings 11.7-8).
In the reign of his son Rehoboam, "There were male cult
prostitutes in the land. They did according to all the abomi-

nations of the nations which Yahweh drove out before the
people of Israel" (1 Kings 14.24). It was in this period that
the Yahwist was writing Genesis. Centuries later Jeremiah
wrote (11.13): "Your gods have become as many as your cities,
O Judah: and as many as the streets of Jerusalem are the
altars you have set up to shame." It is interesting to notice
that it was only after the return to Mesopotamia in the
Babylonian Captivity that we find the Jewish people at last
unalterably monotheist. So in the end Rebekah might feel
that she had been vindicated.

III

Our interest in the myths has been for what they have to say
of the beginning of the universe, this as a preparation for
the study of Genesis. Its opening words are "In the beginning
God . . ."—close enough, the Gentiles might have felt, to
their own "In the beginning a god . . ." But what did the
myth-makers think the gods were? We remind ourselves that
the poets did not create the myths, they made their own use
of myths already there, and the pagan poets can mislead us
as seriously as Milton misleads us in *Paradise Lost* and Dante
in the *Inferno*. Our question concerns the actual myths. Even
there we are forced to limit ourselves: the origins of the
myths are beyond our gaze, if not beyond our guess. Was
the inexplicable, the mysterious, the sacred, the first category
of all? Did the divine precede the gods? Was a periodic ending and re-creation of the universe seen as the nature of
reality before vegetation was seen as its symbol? Such questions are not for us. Our concern is with the myth fully
formed as worshippers accepted and lived it: what did *they*
think the gods were?

Reading the myths, we are forced to shed a vast amount of what to us is of the essence of God. Eternity, for instance. Their gods had a beginning and might have an end. Yet about the beginning, at least, we need not to be too absolute. There *was* a first god.

They had not the concept of self-existence; but in the recurrent idea of the first god bringing himself into existence, they are feeling for it. Their sense that the gods themselves were not assured of endless existence probably flowed not so much from what they thought the gods were as from a sense of insecurity in relation to life and the cosmos: all had come from a primeval chaos, and chaos always threatened. All the mythologies had it: in Canaan, for instance, the conflict between Baal and Mot, the god of evil and all that was sterile, was continuous, victory passing from one to the other and back again, with no certainty of the end.

Meanwhile, apart from any final return of chaos, individual gods could be killed, though only by other gods or the impersonal might of nature, not by men. The gods were personal: to that extent they were like men, but, in ways the myths never defined, superior to men—super-men perhaps? The idea probably varied from worshipper to worshipper, there was no "orthodox" answer. At their grossest, super or not, they were appalling.

There was no answer binding on all the mythologies or on all the individuals within any one system. Each would make its own selection of the human qualities it valued most, and "see" the gods accordingly. There were two qualities in which life was seen at its most vital—power and sexuality. Of these two, individually and in an endless variety of combinations, the myths were made.

It was man's response to power which caused the changes we have noted in all our mythologies, by which the high

gods as they grew older were still reverenced but the gods
that mattered were the dynamic younger ones, Ptah and
Amun and Horus and Set, Marduk, Baal. But the power of
the gods was not limitless; they were not omnipotent even
when that word was used of them. In the Sumerian epic of
Gilgamesh the gods were described as terrified by the Flood,
"cowering like dogs, crouched against the outer wall of
heaven." This, we may feel, is the poet's invention, not the
myth-maker's: and the fear of Tiamat and her monsters
shown by the Sumerian gods in the *Enuma elish* may be
meant solely as a contrast to Babylonian Marduk's courage.

But in none of the mythologies is there an omnipotent
god in the Judaeo-Christian sense. And in the Mesopotamian
we have the clearest awareness of a law or principle of order
fixed at creation from which even the gods were not wholly
exempt. The annual recitation of the Marduk epic of creation was one expression of this. The story of the punishment
of Enlil by the gods is another. We have already noted his
raping of the child goddess Ninlil. The child's plea—"My
vagina is too little, it cannot copulate"—is as touching as
anything in literature. It did not touch Enlil: he forced himself upon her.

With this story we are brought to the second human quality to be divinized, sexuality. It was, of course, linked with
power: it was linked with fruitfulness, too, and so with the
fertility of the earth. When a people settled down in one
area, as Christopher Dawson reminds us, the earth took the
place of animals as the prime reality, and whatever reverence
might be paid to sky gods, the Earth Mother was the one
who must at every cost be placated. There had to be fertility
rites, and these had to be largely sexual. The scholars seem
to agree in thinking that in the beginning the creator gods
were bisexual—either hermaphrodite or able to change from

male to female at will. It was only at a later stage of the myth
that a given god settled on one sex and was shown with a
consort of the other. In any event the male sex organ was
more important than the sexes.

The last thing, I imagine, that a modern would expect to
find issuing from sex held sacred is the significance seen in
castration. That Zeus should castrate his father Uranus as a
way of ensuring his own supremacy is at least comprehensible
(part of the phallus fell into the sea, and from the splash of
its falling came the lovely Aphrodite, "the foam-born"). But
Canaan's high god El castrates not only his father but himself; fertility seems to have demanded castration as it demanded the death of its goddess's husband or lover—Cybele's
Attis, Astarte's Adonis. There was an instinctive sense of the
insecurity of all things, and at every level the feeling that
nothing short of life destroyed would give life hope of
survival.

Whatever came of it, there was a nobility in seeing sex as
sacred (which of course it is: if it were not, it could not be
desecrated). In figures of gods and goddesses the sexual parts
were shown enormous. The Egyptian could cry to Amun,
"Exalted be thy phallus!" That we should be moved to mirth
by this cry does not mean necessarily that we have advanced
beyond his simplicity. In intent, ritual prostitution was an
act of religion not of lust, just as human sacrifice, even on
the horrifying Aztec level, was an act of religion not of blood-
lust. The orgies were meant to be carried through in deadly
seriousness, not licentiously: the most chaste wife felt no
shame, the most proprietary husband no jealousy. There was
no self-consciousness between mistress and servant who had
coupled during the orgy, no craving set up between any two.
In theory none of this would have arisen. The orgiasts were—
not out of this world exactly, but outside time: they were
acting, living, the primeval chaos: what happened had no

bearing on, no continuation in, their daily life. The orgy over, life ran on in its normal course.

That, at least, was the principle. How was it in fact? I do not know what evidence there is. The deeply religious man may have been thus lifted out of himself, and the deeply religious woman. But in any religion (our own quite notably) the deeply religious are in a minority. (We know that there were sceptics, in Egypt certainly, who if they took their part in the rituals, must have done so cynically.) Ritual carries with it a high possibility of lust, as ritual blood-shedding carries a near-certainty of blood-thirstiness. And nothing in what we read of those early pagans suggests that their religions escaped either danger.

Yet we must constantly remind ourselves that for all the continuity of human nature, we are not they. Consider, for example, the frequency with which, in Syria and Asia Minor especially, priests of the Earth goddess were eunuchs. One explanation is that this was a transference into cult and liturgy of the simple fact that the earth yielded its fruit through the labor of oxen, castrated bulls. All this is a reminder of how steadily the early worshippers kept their gaze on the universe, seeing its law as the law of all life, human and divine. The place of cruelty in the myths and the rites is similarly their transferring of the cruelty they saw in nature. In this matter of cruelty, what is strange is the frequency with which the really ferocious one was the goddess —Hathor in Egypt, Tiamat and Inanna in Mesopotamia, Astarte and Anath in Canaan. Had they found this too in nature, or is it simply that the myths were made and written about by men?

One story of Inanna and two of Anath are worth a glance, not only for the cruelty shown but for the light shed on other elements of religion and life—the early divinizing of kings, the diminishing of the first gods by more vigorous descend-

ants, and the continuing warfare of fertility and sterility as
part of the greater war waged by chaos against order.

Inanna (Ishtar to the Accadians) was goddess of love. She
was tortured and killed, but in the Lower World she came
alive and returned, accompanied by demons, to Erech, where
her husband Dumuzi was king (we meet him in the Bible as
Tammuz). Because he had rejoiced in her own torture and
death, she has the demons take him to the Lower World. He
used to be thought one of the vegetation gods who died and
returned with the seasons. But recent scholarship has established that there is no return for him. Nor could there be—
Inanna's husband was whoever became king of Erech: each
new king was wedded to the goddess, a temple prostitute
taking her place in the wedding.

Anath, sister and consort of Baal, is quite especially mon-
strous, wading in the blood of her victims, "swelling her
liver with laughter." Determined that the high-god El shall
give her husband Baal a palace worthy of him, she threatens
that she will

> "trample El like a sheep on the ground
> make his gray hair flow with blood
> the gray of his beard with gore."

El's comment is "I know thee to be impetuous, O my daugh-
ter."[9]

Naturally she takes part in the conflict between Baal and
Mot. In what we are tempted to think of as one round in
that never-ending fight, she seizes Mot—

> With a sword she cleaves him
> with a fan she winnows him

> *with a fire she burns him*
> *with a millstone she grinds him*
> *in the field she plants him.*[10]

With Mot thus disposed of, she raises Baal to life. But of course Mot comes back and the war continues.

Where in all this can we find a beginning of monotheism? Nowhere perhaps: only a feeling, in the more sophisticated, of the unsatisfactoriness, even irksomeness, of polytheism. To have one god supreme, with universal dominion, as against the specialized powers of the others, was normal. But the tendency grew to see these others as the supreme god manifesting himself in them for special purposes. Beyond the powers shown as Marduk's in the Fifty Names with which the *Enuma elish* concludes, there are not many powers left to other gods. In the Cossaean form of the myth, Marduk appears as identical with each of the male gods. And Albright tells of devotees of the war god Ninnurta who saw all the parts of his body as the gods and goddesses of Babylon's pantheon—his two eyes Enlil and Ninlil, his chin Ishtar, his neck Marduk.

As between peoples it was natural enough to identify the gods of one's own list with the equivalent gods of another. Round 1320—as part of the explosion following Akhenaton's effort to concentrate worship on the solar disk—the Pharaohs treated the god Set as supreme. The Hyksos identified Set with their own Baal, Isis or Hathor with Astarte, and so on. In a treaty Rameses II made with the Hittites, the chief male deities of Asia and Syria are actually called Set.

The increasing emphasis on one god would have meant a movement towards monotheism. But the interchangeability had as one effect the diminution—at least for the educated—

of the sense of true personality, and the movement seems to have been in the direction of pantheism. The personality of the divine was the decisive test. It still is.

For all the joy I find in Genesis, it is with reluctance that I leave the myths. I find them not only full of instruction about God and man and nature but continually fascinating —as fascinating in their similarities as in their variety. In any given system, somebody must have actually composed the myth. It utters a way of seeing, feeling, reacting common to a whole group, but somebody uttered it; and other somebodies worked on it, improving it, worsening it perhaps: the collective mind may condition it, demand it, respond to it, but cannot compose and utter it.

And in almost every given system, from China to Peru, from Eskimo to Polynesian, we notice the similarity of the first utterance—one scholar, indeed, has complained of their "monotony." The almost universal reaction to the seen, heard, smelt, felt universe is that it is not only not the whole story, it is not even the main part of it. There is an unseen, unheard, unsmelt, unfelt reality, superior to it, supporting it: this was what the myth expressed: the rituals expressed the universal desire to be in right relation to it, the almost universal desire to communicate with it. They did not consciously argue that because the world about them is as it is and things happen as they do, therefore there must be powers behind the world, prior to the happenings. They seem not to have had even a beginning of Apologetics or any need for it. The myth carried its own conviction. But from that first root of similarity, what dazzling varieties of religious beliefs and practices have grown, whole forests of them, jungles of them. Is Christianity simply one more? I cannot hope to settle the question for anyone but myself. I simply note down my own thought upon it.

In the study of Comparative Religion men can deceive themselves by listing elements of similarity without sufficient reference to the totality in which these elements have their existence, from which they draw their meaning. One man observes, for instance, that fakirs in India and monks in the West inflict pain upon their bodies and assumes that asceticism is one indifferentiated reality everywhere; actually the two asceticisms are poles apart, the one arising from contempt of the body and desire to be rid of it, the other in a desire to reduce the appetites of the body to control, that it may be a fit partner of the spirit in the everlasting life for which both alike are destined. Or again one has seen sacraments equated with magic—but magic is an attempt to find the right words or material things to impose one's own will upon the material universe in order to get material results, while sacraments use matter in obedience to God's instruction and the results aimed at are spiritual.

A third instance out of hundreds: the priests of the Earth Mother were often eunuchs; the great Christian thinker Origen castrated himself; worshippers of Attis would run round the streets waving a sword, their frenzy increasing till they castrated themselves. All three have a connection with religion but are otherwise wholly different. The reason for the eunuch priests we have already considered; Origen acted, as he later saw, from a misunderstanding of Christ's words about those "who make themselves eunuchs for the sake of the kingdom of heaven"; the Attis people were acting in sheer frenzied worship of the castrated Attis. In *The Golden Bough,* Frazer compares them with Catholic nuns who voluntarily choose chastity.

My own conviction is that the religion Christ brought is unique among religions rather in the way that man is unique among animals. Elements of the human body are to be found in animals, even hints towards the human mind; animals are

rough sketches of man's body, barely even rough sketches of
man's mind—naturally, since animals were evolving towards
man, not vice versa. Similarly, elements of Christianity are
to be found in all the mythologies. Christ is what they were
feeling towards, fumbling towards, the answer to all their
questions and the fulfillment of all their needs; the answer
to questions they had never thought to ask, the fulfillment
of needs they had never arrived at feeling.

A man of genius—insight, sympathy, selective power—
seeking among the paganisms might have built for himself
some dark notion of what the true religion might be like. I
do not mean that such a man could construct Christ's religion in advance, but that when he saw it he would cry out,
That is it!—and could proceed from one element in it to
another saying, *This* they all had; *this* so many were trying
for and all but had; *this* I now see how one or other of them
missed; *this* and *this* and *this* they never conceived—but
without the revelation of Christ how could they?

So I see it—naturally, perhaps; I am a Christian.

NOTES

1. New York, Doubleday, 1961.

2. This translation is in James B. Pritchard, ed., *The Ancient
Near East: An Anthology of Texts and Pictures* (Princeton, N.J.:
Princeton University Press, 1958).

3. These lines are translated by R. T. Rundle Clark in his
Myth and Symbol in Ancient Egypt (New York, Grove Press,
and London, Thames and Hudson, Ltd., 1960).

4. W. F. Albright, *From the Stone Age to Christianity*, 2d ed.
(New York, Doubleday Anchor Book, 1957).

5. These lines and the excerpts from *Enuma Elish* which follow are quoted from the translation in E. A. Speiser, *Ancient*

Near East Texts (Princeton, N.J.: Princeton University Press, 1950).

6. *Ibid.*

7. *Patterns in Comparative Religion* (New York, Sheed and Ward, 1958), p. 421.

8. Speiser, *op. cit.*

9. Quoted in Albright, *From the Stone Age to Christianity.*

10. *Ibid.*

3

Creation Revealed

SIMPLY AS IT STANDS, the first chapter of Genesis sounds ridiculous—with the world created in six days six thousand years ago, man created in one crowded day upon an earth only a few days older, the earth lying in its flatness between the mass of water below itself (which came up as rivers) and the mass of water above the sky (which came down as rain). Merely to write that sentence reminds us of an age that has passed, the age of the novelty of Evolution.

It is all dead enough now. People accept Evolution as a fact but are no longer thrilled by it, or even greatly interested. Those who carry their thinking beyond today's pleasures and today's problems have come to the conclusion that where the human race is going matters more than where it comes from. It is the mood of the Isaiah phrase "Do not remember the things of the past, for I will show you new wonders." People are seeing "new wonders" that Isaiah never dreamed of, though there is not much of a tendency to connect them with Isaiah's God.

All that remains of the Evolution conflict is a general feeling that religion fought against science and lost. As we look back on it, the conflict seems comic. The fossils were a horrid problem to the believer, till someone advanced the theory that God had put them there to test our faith. I remember how pleased I was with so conclusive a solution. I was eleven when I heard it.

There should never have been a conflict, of course. The writer of Genesis was not concerned with the age of the world and had no thought of mentioning it. His concern was with the relation of man to God—the fact note, not the date: the fact is vitally important, the date not very. Only minds profoundly uninterested in the profound questions which Genesis does treat could think that either the "when" of man's creation or the "how" of the creative process mattered more. In comparison they hardly matter at all. Yet the when and the how were what the conflict between the scientists and the fundamentalists was mainly about. To the writer of the opening chapter of Genesis, the findings of modern geology would have been fascinating no doubt, but not embarrassing.

To believers the chapter *is* embarrassing, but only if it is taken literally. A first-rate statement by a fundamentalist, who takes it literally and is not embarrassed, is *Genes, Genesis and Evolution* by John W. Klotz, a biologist and Protestant pastor. To me it seems quite clear that the Genesis writer did not mean it literally. He had certain vastly important truths to utter, he set them in this particular framework; but the truths were his theme, not the framework. As the Biblical Commission told Cardinal Suhard in 1948: "They relate in simple and figurative language, adapted to the understanding of mankind at a lower stage of development, the fundamental truths underlying the divine scheme of salvation, as well as a popular description of the origins of the human race and of the chosen people."

Nor need we think this a desperate excuse to cover the no longer deniable fact that geology has disproved Genesis! In the third century Origen had asked "what rational creature" would believe that there was a first, second and third day before the sun was made. And fifteen centuries before Darwin and the Geologists, St. Augustine wrote *De Genesi ad litteram* to show that the account of creation could not possibly have been meant by the writer to be taken literally. The six days allotted to creation, for example, were symbolic, and he has two different theories of what they symbolized. His general notion, set out in Books XI and XII of the *Confessions,* was that God created in one single act all the elements which later, in the unhurrying pace of the ages, would develop into the universe we know. It was Augustine who said, "What do I care if the heavens are a circumambient sphere, and not a sort of dishcover?" Aquinas has something similar in mind when he writes: "The treatment of creation in Genesis is logical and not chronological" (*De Potentia,* q. 4, art. 2, ad 2). In the twelfth century, roughly midway between Augustine and Darwin, Andrew of St. Victor anticipated the Biblical Commission—the Genesis story had been written, he said, for the instruction of people in a state of ignorance.

The writer wanted to tell of one God, a being of limitless intelligence and power, by whom all things whatsoever had been created. So he gives us a psalm, or hymn, of creation, bringing in earth and sea and sky, sun and moon, sea animals and land animals and man, with man coming last as that towards which the process was directed; and he divides the whole according to the seven days of the Hebrew week, Sabbath rest and all. He was not trying to give the order of creation but only its total inclusiveness—in the next chapter, written centuries earlier and certainly known to him, man is spoken of as appearing before the animals; neither of the writers thought he actually knew the order or that it mattered.

The Hymn is constructed with great art. It would have been hard to sketch in more rapidly the stage on which the drama of man's earthly life was to be acted. Yet that is the least part of the writer's achievement. Consider what, in that brief space, he was asserting and what he was denying.

God was Someone, not just a force; he was distinct from the universe—as against pantheism; the powers of nature and all living things were his creatures (it is hard to imagine how shocked millions must have been to find the sun, their supreme god, thus casually brought into the picture halfway through as a convenience thought up for man by Israel's God and not even named—sun and moon being simply "lights to separate the day from the night"). He was one, as against the myriad polytheisms; evil was not only not a separate creative principle, as dualism held, it is given no part at all either in the production of the universe by God or in the universe as God produced it; the universe as it came from God was "very good"—this against the vast Eastern tendency to write down matter as evil or illusion: we tend to associate this with Plato, who was not yet born when the first chapter of Genesis was written, but the idea was already there, in the Hindus, for instance, and in the Persians, to whom the Jews had been brought close by their captivity in Babylon. No: for our writer the universe was good.

And man was to be its Lord—no myth had ever approached that.

The whole thing is a masterpiece of economy, economy which a commentary cannot hope to match—so much that the writer took for granted we have to explain, so much of what was in the back of his mind or even the front we have

to guess, what he writes must be tested in the light of so
many things that we know and he did not.

I IN THE BEGINNING

In the beginning God created the heavens and
the earth.

This is how the book of Genesis—the beginning—begins. In
the ten words of its opening sentence—eight in Hebrew—
more is contained than had ever been uttered in a single
sentence, more than ever would be uttered in a single sentence till John wrote the opening words of his Gospel—"In
the beginning was the Word, and the Word was with God
and the Word was God." The depths of what each is saying
are beyond our reach, beyond their writers' reach too. The
Genesis man, for instance, could have had no notion that
John's sentence lies hidden in his own. Even the surface—
what each realized he was saying—needs exploring. John's
sentence we shall study in a Postscript. Here we explore the
Genesis assertion that nothing whatever exists apart from the
will of God that it should be.

God: The myths do not issue from, or even issue into,
monotheism; henotheism is as close as they came, one supreme god. As we have seen, one of the Pharaohs, Akhenaton,
asserted his belief in one absolute God to be pictured solely
by the sun's disk. His "reform" did not survive in Egypt.
Polytheism was not to be killed by royal decree, its roots
went too deep, into the centuries and into the nature of man.
The Jews did not at once get it totally out of their system.
It was in the Babylonian Captivity, seven hundred years after
Moses, that they became finally monotheist. "I am the Lord

that made all things and there is none with me." So said
Isaiah (44.6). So said the Hymn of Creation.

The God of Genesis has no mythology, no background,
no relation with other gods, no pre-history of any kind. He
is simply there. What he might have done before the creation
of the universe is not discussed; there is no hint of what
might have concerned him apart from men and their doings;
until near the end of the Old Testament no inquiry into
what life of his own he might have: he is not a vegetation
god, and though later in Scripture there will be many mani-
festations of him in the skies, he is not a sky god. Nor did he
need to be accounted for. The bare possibility of his not
existing would not have occurred to our writer. Three centuries later the writer of the *Wisdom of Solomon* could speak
of men who were ignorant of God: but he wrote in Greek
and had read the Greek philosophers. He condemns them
as "foolish by nature: for they were unable from the good
things that are seen to know him who exists . . . they supposed that either fire or wind or swift air [Anaximenes
thought air] or the circle of the stars or turbulent water
[Thales of Miletus chose water] were the gods that rule the
world."

But this was later. It may be doubted if any of the earlier
Jewish writers had ever met an atheist. Their world was filled
with the myths and with the rituals which expressed them;
only the rarest person, one imagines, ever said, "But how do
we know?" In neither Testament is there any effort to set
out a proof that God exists. Genesis 1, for example, was not
arguing from the order of the universe to the necessity of a
creator. It is one more expression of the almost universal
feeling that the visible was not the whole story, that there
was Something beyond, Something other. The visible universe did not "prove" the existence of that other, it simply
carried the other with it. The self which was aware of the

visible was as aware of the invisible. The most the visible
could do was give clues to the nature of the other. "The
heavens show forth"—not the existence but—"the glory of
the Lord" (Ps. 19.1,D).[1]

In the first chapter, God is *Elohim*. In the next two *Yahweh Elohim*. Some think this Elohim was not in the original.
Certainly in the next seven chapters, from Adam to Abram
(with whom we enter history proper) God is Yahweh. *Elohim*
simply means god—a kind of common noun! The root is El,
used for god by Semitic peoples generally. Elohim, the special
word of the Hebrews, is peculiar in itself since it is plural in
form (from Eloah) but, when used for the one God, takes a
verb in the singular. This usage did not begin with the
Chosen People, the Canaanites already had it. To give a word
of exceptional richness a plural form while keeping the meaning singular was not unknown—it was not only so with "god"
but with "blood" and "life." Yahweh is a proper noun, the
personal name of the Elohim of the Jews. There is argument
as to the meaning of the word. It is a form of the verb "to
be"—that is fairly generally assumed, but nothing else is.
The likeliest meaning seems to be "I am." It is the first word
of the phrase "Yahweh ashur Yiweh" (Ex. 3.14). I discuss it
lengthily in *God and the Human Mind*. God had com-
manded Moses to bring the Israelites out of Egypt; Moses
replies that the Israelites would demand the name of the
God who sent him. And God said, "Yahweh ashur Yihweh.
Say to the people of Israel, Yahweh has sent me to you."

Primitively the Jews may have seen Yahweh as essentially
their god—each people had its Elohim, theirs was more powerful than the others. They came to know that Yahweh *is*
Elohim, but a genuine distinction remained in their minds,
not unlike the distinction between the words "Christ" and
"Jesus." Christ—the Messiah, the Anointed—expresses the

nature and function; when the Christ came into the world
his personal name was Jesus; only slowly does the word
Christ, too, become a personal name. Similarly Elohim is
God, transcendent, omnipotent: the creation of the whole
universe is his work: the first chapter of Genesis is all of
Elohim. Yahweh is his personal name, to be used of God as
personally experienced—as present to his chosen people or
to chosen individuals.

Yet the distinction is not cast-iron. Eve says at Seth's birth:
"*Elohim* has appointed for me another child" (Gen. 4.25):
Enoch walked with *the Elohim* after the birth of Methuselah
(5.22); Noah found favor with *Yahweh* (6.8). Jacob at Bethel
(the house of El) made his vow: "If Elohim will be with me
. . . Yahweh shall be my Elohim" (Gen. 28.20).

It does not seem thinkable that a writer should invariably
use one only of these words. The probability is surely that
he could move as easily between Elohim and Yahweh as we
from Christ to Our Lord, to Jesus Christ, to Jesus. Yet somewhat as Catholics utter the name Jesus rarely and bow as
they utter it, so to the Jews Yahweh was a name pronounced
only once in the year, and that by the high priest in the
Holy of Holies, where none could hear but God; even in
writing, only the consonants Y H W H appeared. It may be
that each attitude results from a text narrowly understood—
the one from "You shall not take the name of the Lord your
God in vain" (Ex. 20.7), the other from "At the name of
Jesus every knee should bow" (Phil. 2.10).

As things have turned out, it is Elohim which survives in
Christian usage—we pray to God and speak of God as *God*
—only rarely and rhetorically as Jehovah (an odd coined
word), never as Yahweh. The reason, of course, is not any
special sense of ineffability about the word Yahweh, but that
it meets no present need. A special function of a personal
name is to distinguish one individual from another of the

same nature or species: with monotheism so established that polytheism does not exist even as a memory in us, the individual name lost its point. "God" was sufficient. There is only one.

In the beginning: the Hebrew word is *bereshith,* a strong word; not just any beginning, it goes to the root of something that matters.

The writer need not have been thinking of origin in time, a first moment before which there was no time and no universe. The words need mean no more than that the world owes its origin to God, all that it has is by his gift. Dependence is the point rather than origin.

Time measures the changes of the material universe, so that time and the universe exist together. If there were no universe, there would be no changes to measure, no time therefore. In other words, time is not a river ever flowing (any more than space is an ocean always there) into which the universe was suddenly dropped, or out of which it suddenly popped. In that sense there never was a time when the universe did not exist. Time is like the ticking of the universe—no universe, no tick: but was there a first tick?

Thomas Aquinas held, to the fury of Bonaventure, that reason cannot prove that the material universe had a beginning, that only this first verse of Genesis settles the matter for us. But does it? Does it say that time had a beginning, so that the universe has existed for a countable number of years?—not necessarily countable by men, of course, but countable in its own nature since it started from zero and proceeded year by year.

The Fourth Council of the Lateran, quoted by Vatican I, says that God "at the beginning of time simultaneously established of nothing both the spiritual and the material creation." "At the beginning of time" may mean, probably

does, that the created universe had a beginning, a first moment before which it did not exist. But the Council may have
meant only to deny the Albigensian teaching that prior to
creation there were centuries of uncreated existence.

What of "simultaneously"? The Latin is *simul* from the
Vulgate translation of Sirach 17.1—"creavit omnia simul."
But the Greek word is *koine,* which means "equally"; i.e.,
there is nothing not created by God.

Created: The word is used three times in the Hymn—for
the heavens and the earth, for living things, and for man.

The Hebrew verb *bara* is used close on fifty times in Scripture, always of God's activity, and always of something that
only God could do—e.g., "Then the Lord will create over
the whole of Mount Zion and over her assemblies a cloud by
day, and the smoke and the shining of a flaming fire by night"
(Is. 4.5). But *bara* does not of itself mean making of nothing,
making without the use of matter already there. That that
was how the Jews came to read Genesis is clear from the
second book of Macchabees (7.28): six brothers had been
slain by Antiochus, who tried to win over the seventh: their
mother said to the last of her sons: "Look at the heavens and
the earth and see everything that is in them, and realize that
God did not make them out of things that existed." Only
one who had read the Greek philosophers would have
phrased it like that, but it adds nothing to "God created the
heavens and the earth," i.e. everything.

Paul is as direct as Macchabees—"The God in whom
Abraham believed gives life to the dead and calls into existence the things that do not exist" (Rom. 4.17). And
Hebrews (11.3) suggests a further element—"By faith we
understand that the world was created by the word [*hremate,*
the uttered word] of God, that what is seen is made out of

things *which do not appear*," which seems to imply that they exist in the mind of God.

Professor Pelikan says that Theophilus of Antioch was the first Church Father to assert creation from nothing—the matter from which God made and shaped the world had in some manner been created by him. For an official assertion of *ex nihilo* we have to await the Fourth Council of the Lateran— I have just quoted it.

Is this the Self-Existent Being? Hebrew had no word for being, no word for *existence*. The Jews did not isolate existence as a distinct concept. They took it totally for granted. It was just too universal to be noticed. Everything that exists has existence, so to speak. (Much as we may imagine that no deep-sea fish notices water.) Our writer (and centuries of theologians before him) had thought long on "I am who am" —the Hymn is practically a meditation on it. The writer may never have heard of Self-Existent Being. But he would certainly have denied (1) that God had had to be brought into existence; (2) that any given thing could have existed without God. And with these two denials, there is not much of Self-Existent Being left unaffirmed.

What Genesis says here we find again in Isaiah (44.24): "Thus says the Lord your Redeemer who formed you from the womb: I am the Lord who made all things, who stretched out the heavens alone, who spread out the earth—who was with me?"

The heavens and the earth. Hebrew has a way of expressing totality by linking two polar opposites—e.g., "the living and the dead" meant "everyone"; "neither in this world nor in the world to come" meant "never." Having no word for cosmos, the Jews used "the heavens and the earth" to mean the whole universe, everything.

Observe how matter-of-fact our writer is. Others might be
lyrical about creation, not he. The book of Job (38.4-7), for
example, has God say: "Were you there when I laid the
foundations of the world . . . when the morning stars sang
together and all the sons of God shouted for joy?" This is
not the Priest's way of speech. He is terse and businesslike;
one can imagine him as answering God's question "Were you
there?" with a single word—"No." He was not there when
the world's foundations were laid. So he states the fact of
creation without adornment.

The heavens and the earth were made by God—not from
or out of God. Still less was God produced from, or in any
way emergent from, them. They needed to be accounted for,
God did not.

> The earth was formless and void [tohu wa-bohu],
> and darkness covered the face of the deep [to
> hom]; and the Spirit of God was moving over
> the face of the waters.

Is the writer saying that this was what God created "in the
beginning," then in six days forming from it the universe as
we know it? The second Gamaliel (A.D. 100) taught that God
created "tohu and bohu, darkness, wind, water and the
abyss." But most writers now seem to think that the words
are an effort to say, or rather to picture or somehow convey,
what precedes the creative action which produced our universe. If so, what do they say, or picture, or convey? Formless,
void, dark: to a people who had not the concept of nothingness, this triple absence, of form and content and light, would
be a good way of conveying it. It was a good way, anyhow,
of conveying chaos: and creation was imagined, in that day,
as a passage not from nonexistence to existence, but from
chaos to ordered existence.

For the modern scientist all life began in the sea. An apologist of the older sort might have quoted this (had he known it) to show how God inspired the Genesis writer to use a phrase which long after would prove to be in accord with the findings of science. In fact it was a nod to the myths. Both in Egypt and Mesopotamia, life begins in a watery waste, inert, lifeless. There is the same idea in Indian mythology of a primal ocean, Vishnu in one story appearing upon it as a child on a banyan leaf, in another as a cosmic dreamer on the coils of a serpent. This the Priest may not have known, but the myths closer at hand he knew well, especially the Mesopotamian. Where no point of principle was involved, he used the framework of the universe and the order of its coming to be which his ancestors had learnt from them. Much of what they contained he rejected, not by direct denial but by so stating the truth that the false would be seen as false. The great positive values in the myths he used, enhancing their value by placing them in the context of reality. And he responded with delight, surely, to elements in them which approached, even when they did not quite attain, the fullness of the truth he knew.

Of this last we have an example here. In the Hermopolis form of the Egyptian myth, Nun, the inert waste of waters, was stirred to activity by Amun, god of air or wind, moving across it. The Priest might have been pleased to meet this particular story very much as we, though we know that Isaiah's "Holy, Holy, Holy" no more means the Trinity than does the Genesis phrase "They saw three and adored one," are still pleased to come across phrasings so apt to the doctrine. The Genesis writer was as capable as we of seeing the contradiction in the myth—for Amun himself would not have existed at all unless Nun had had enough activity to produce him. But in his own rendering (the same verb is used in "the Spirit of God, *ruah Elohim,* was moving over the face of the

waters") there was no contradiction. The myth of a god
emerging from the waters had no application to the God of
Israel.

But the Amun myth may have a bearing on the translation
of *ruah Elohim. Ruah* means both "wind" and "spirit"—in
its first meaning "wind," then "spirit" as also being at once
invisible and powerful. But grammatically *elohim* here could
be either the possessive of the noun—"of God"—or an adjective—"godlike," awe-inspiring, beyond the natural. Many
scholars prefer to read it as an adjective—Speiser, for instance, has "awesome wind." And one remembers the "strong
wind" blowing from the east which divided the sea in order
that Israel might cross to safety (Ex. 14.21). Nothing essential seems to be involved. For myself (and for the *Revised
Standard Version* and the *Jerusalem Bible*) "Spirit of God"
seems likely here. In the Hymn of Creation, "Elohim" is
used thirty times—twenty-nine times clearly for "God." It
would seem odd if this one time it should not, especially as
in the Egyptian myth it *was* a god who stirred the waters:
and the verb here translated "moving" is used in Deuteronomy 32.11 to compare God guarding Israel with a mother
eagle hovering over its young. That the Spirit of God should
be hovering over the waste of waters has a richness of meaning. That a strong wind should be blowing over it seems to
be only a climatic detail with no present significance and
no sequel.

It is possible that the Priest had the Babylonian myths in
mind when he chose *tohu wa-bohu* as the phrase for formless
and void. Add an *-m* to each and you have *Tohum* which
might be Tiamat, *Bohum* which *might* be Scripture's monster Behemoth (monsters being Tiamat's special contribution). But there are those who think *bohu* comes from Baau,
a Phoenician goddess of the night. It is possible that when he
said "darkness was upon the face of *the deep*"—in Hebrew,

te hom—he again had Tiamat in mind. If so, he could hardly
have shown more clearly how far superior was God—
serenely moving or hovering over the face of the waters—to
Tiamat, to Enki who was afraid of her, to Marduk who de-
ceived and slew her. But if there are such etymological con-
nections, they belong to a far past. The words themselves
had become part of the language, used with as little consciousness of the original root as we have of the sacrifice of
the Mass when we speak of Christmas. Sumerian Tiamat has
about as much relevance in the present context as Phoenician
Baau. As Father Alexander Jones says, the myths receded,
leaving their phrases behind.

The study of ancient languages has almost remade Scripture scholarship: even to translate the words of Christ back
into Aramaic brings to light meanings or emphases lost in
Greek, and lost all over again in English. But, like all good
things, linguistic and philosophical study has its perils. In
particular it is a temptation for scholars to pounce upon verbal resemblances and build towering constructions upon
them.

If our civilization should be all but annihilated in the next
war, one can imagine a scholar two thousand years from now
discovering that as late as the twentieth century we still called
the planets by the names of Roman gods, and arguing from
this that we still worshipped them: he could quote in support our use of adjectives like jovial, mercurial, martial—
to say nothing of venereal. Another scholar would discover
not only that we were still calling the days of the week by
the names of German gods, but that Saturn was in both
lists, the days and the planets, and that, as a tribute doubtless
to the Egyptians, we started our week with the Sun. He
might think all this evidence of Ecumenism, if civilization
had by this time re-progressed so far as Ecumenism.

Glance again at Israel's "subjection" to Mesopotamian

c

myths. Here is Isaiah (23.12): "He shall stretch over it the
line of confusion (*tohu*) and the plummet of chaos (*bohu*)
and all her princes shall be nothing (*ephes*)." Tohu and Bohu
we have seen as (possibly) Tiamat and Behemoth (or Baau).
And Ephes? Clearly Apsu, Tiamat's husband slain by Enki.
Professor Albright warns us: "Biblical handbooks are clut-
tered with false etymologies, as well as with correct etymologies from which erroneous and indemonstrable deductions
are made."[2] (Philology needs to be both cleansed and enriched by archaeology, to say nothing of common sense.)

We can find the same words used. But if we move from
words to what the words are saying, then to come from the
myths (great as their positive values are) to the first chapter
of Genesis is like waking out of a nightmare into daylight.
The heart of the difference lies in this, that the Genesis
writer did not get his religion from the myths, but from the
revelation of God. The myths arose from men's experience
of the universe, but Genesis from the Israelite experience of
God in the Sinai desert on which they had had seven or
eight hundred years to meditate, and from the continuing
action of God in their history since. Secure in that, the
writer could use the insights of the myths and their very
words in total confidence. A modern unbeliever can say that
the idea of the wind moving over the waste of waters was
later spiritualized into God. To which the Genesis writer
would have happily assented—he now knew God as the
myth-maker did not.

Israel in short did not get its religion, any more than the
Greeks got their philosophy, simply by refining the myths.
Both de-mythologized. The Greeks did it for themselves by
looking searchingly at nature, to de-personalize it. Israel did
it by listening to a God genuinely personal. Both could make
their own use of the myths—the Jews more easily and richly

than the Greeks, because they had a religion of whose revelation by God they were wholly convinced: it would not have
occurred to them to say of God what Aristotle said of Zeus,
that it would be ridiculous to talk of loving him.

And God said, "Let there be. . . ."

The Hymn divides into eight acts the six-day production
of the totality of things, from light to Man. Each is introduced by "And God said," each closed by "And it was so."

God said. Knowing what we now know, we cannot help
recalling the opening of John's Gospel—"In the beginning
was the word . . . all things were made by him." That is not
what the writer of Genesis was saying, of course; yet we can
rejoice in the aptness of what he did say, just as he might
have rejoiced in the aptness of Egypt's Amun moving over
the inert waste to stir it to activity. The Priest had not read
John; but John had read the Priest, and in the opening of
his Gospel clearly remembered those earlier opening words.
So perhaps may Mary of Nazareth have remembered them
when she said, "Be it done unto me according to thy
word."

Creation by a word is found in the Egyptian myths. The
Memphis god Ptah created each thing by uttering its name.
The god Khepri created himself by uttering his own name.
The Egyptians had a religious respect for the power, the
magic power perhaps, of the word: but it was a spoken word,
a word sounded, not simply the will of the god but its spoken-
ness. By "said" our writer meant the word formed in the
mind, needing no mechanism of lungs and air and tongue

and lips: the God of Israel was not of that sort. As the psalm-
ist was to say, "He spoke and they were made" (148.5), clari-
fied for us by two of Paul's phrases—God "accomplished all
things according to the counsel of his will" (Eph. 1.11) and
"He can send his call to that which has no being, as if it
already were" (Rom. 4.17, K).[3]

After each of the creative acts introduced by "And God
said," there is "And it was so." As we come from the myths,
nothing impresses us more in Genesis than the absence of
conflict. To quote from Mircea Eliade's *Patterns in Comparative Religion*: in the myths the cosmos is not "created *ex
nihilo* by the supreme divinity, but comes into existence by
means of the sacrifice (or self-sacrifice) of a god, a primeval
monster, of a superman, or a primeval animal."[4] In the
Hymn of Creation there is nothing of this. God does not
strive, he wills.

But the myths are an often magnificent effort to express
reality as men have experienced it. The emergence of life
is real, it is mysterious. The Egyptians found a symbol for
it in the lotus, rooted in mud but opening with the sun's
rising and closing with its setting. The myths of conflict also
try to account for something really there—the precariousness
of things, the threat of inundation renewing primeval chaos,
the gods themselves never sure of survival. Once monotheism
was established and in secure possession, the Jewish writers
could use the mythic imagery to express a sense of resistance
to God as an abiding element in men and things, a nihilism,
a thrusting back towards original nothingness perhaps, almost a craving for it.

This element in creation was symbolized for the Jews by
the sea—agitated, chaotic, destructive, uncontrollable. Close
to the end of the last book of the New Testament we see
how strong the feeling was: "Then I saw a new heaven and

a new earth; for the first heaven and the first earth had passed away, *and the sea was no more.*"

The monsters of the myths were matched by monsters in the sea which could be allegorized—like Leviathan, like Rahab, all violence and defiance. "By his power he stilled the sea, by his understanding he smote Rahab" (Job. 26.12). "Understanding" keeps this close to Genesis 1. But "Thou didst crush the heads of Leviathan" (Ps. 74.13-14) suggests the story found in the Ugarit texts of a god in combat with a seven-headed serpent; and there are strong hints of Marduk and his slaying of Tiamat—"Thou didst cut Rahab in pieces" (Is. 51.9); "Thou didst rule the raging of the sea . . . thou didst crush Rahab like a carcass" (Ps. 89.9-10).

Whether or not we believe in a race psyche, a race unconscious, a race memory, there is certainly a race psychology, psychological needs and ways of acting that go with being men. In all ages and places, to take one example, men need metaphors; and the same metaphors recur, which means that they meet a need, in every age and place. Polynesians, for instance, have legends surprisingly like those of Northern Siberian nomads. The Jews were forbidden to make "graven images"—of God, or "of anything in the heavens above, or the earth beneath, or the waters under the earth." But they could not help wanting metaphors, similes, analogies.

For the Old Testament writers mythology provided apter metaphors than nature could, precisely because it was explicitly religious. In *Peake's Commentary*, S. H. Hooke writes of the probability of the existence under the early Hebrew monarchy of a great New Year festival of the sort that Mesopotamia had and Egypt had not—a dramatic showing of the Kingship of Yahweh and his triumph over the forces of evil. The crushing of Leviathan and the cutting in pieces of Rahab may have been echoes of it. It is not unthinkable that the Hymn of Creation gives us its "program."

II LET THERE BE LIGHT

In the days when Genesis was attacked—and defended—as literal history, there was much mockery of the "statement" that light was made before the sun. Even if the whole thing was figurative, men argued, what purpose could be served by so idiotic a reversal of obvious facts? But the men of Genesis did not see it like that. They knew the sun as the most luminous of all light's bearers, but not as light's source. After all, there was light on days when the sun was not to be seen! Indeed there were pagans who thought the Moon god more valuable than the divine Sun. For the Sun gave light only in the daytime when it was less needed, the Moon at night.

In any event, did the writer think of light here solely as the light we know by the eyes of our body? Possibly. If so, the words he used have in themselves more meaning than he meant. If it is merely chance, it is still splendid chance, that the first words we hear from God are "let there be light," a distant anticipation of the "light from light" with which the Nicene Creed utters the relation of God the Son to God the Father.

What we may call the program or schedule of creation is very carefully structured. In the first three days are produced Night and Day, Sky and Sea, Dry Land: on the next three, each of these is "populated"—with sun and moon and stars; with birds and fish; with animals and man. Each day begins with "And God said, Let . . ." and ends with "There was evening and morning, a second" (or third, or whatever) "day." In between came "And it was so" (or an equivalent phrase), and "God saw that it was good." Nothing could be more clearly liturgical.

It has been said that the order of creation here is "tied" to the order in the Babylonian *Enuma elish*. Why not? As we have noted, the order was not the writer's point but the inclusiveness: one order would do as well as another: to the science of the day this seemed the way things had happened. In any event there were plenty of lists to choose from—for instance, *The Instruction for King Meri-ka-re*, written in Egypt between 2500 and 2000 B.C., has the words with which Genesis begins—"God made heaven and earth." But they are not saying the same thing—"God repelled the water monster. He made the breath of life for their nostrils. They who issued from his body are his images. He arises in heaven according to their desire. He made plants, animals, fish. He makes the light of day."[5]

Genesis' inclusiveness has one element we might not notice. It manages to include all the divinities worshipped by the surrounding peoples (except the serpent, who was already there in Chapter 3). And it shows them not as gods, but as matter called into being by the sole will of the one God, with man to have dominion over them. Thus "He called the dry land earth and the waters the sea" and holds them in the boundaries he has set for them—a way of putting firmly in their place the Ocean god, and the universally worshipped Earth Mother. And whereas in Canaan and in Babylon the sea monsters were the rivals of the gods, in Genesis they are simply large creatures in the sea—"Leviathan which thou didst form to sport in it" (Ps. 104.26): Tiamat's monsters were not sportive.

This first chapter is liturgical, but not mechanical. Every word is weighed. "God saw that it was good" is applied to light, but not to darkness, which has in it an element of the chaos in which the whole process began. One constantly notices points of the sort. Thus, there are so many variations of the creative word:

> Let the waters be gathered . . . dry land appear
> . . . birds fly.
> Let there be light, a firmament, lights in the
> firmament.
> Let the earth put forth vegetation . . . bring
> forth living creatures.
> Let the waters bring forth. . . .

Then, for the only time, "Let us make"—reserved for the making of man.

> Let us make man in our image, after our
> likeness. . . .

Let us make man. As with all the other makings of the Hymn, this one is by God's word. We are not offered anything like his making of men in the *Enuma elish*—Marduk and the rest slew one of the gods, Kingu: they

> *. . . drew off his blood*
> *And of his blood they fashioned mankind.*[6]

There is not even the dust of the earth from which man is formed, or the breathing by which he becomes a living soul, in Genesis 2.

The "us" is curious. The writer is so very monotheist, and Hebrew has no royal (or editorial) "we." The Dominican scholar Père Lagrange suggests that the writer is conscious of such a fullness of being in God that he can think of him as deliberating with himself in the same way as a number of men might. Would this perhaps argue a degree of philosophizing about the nature of God improbable in a Jew of that period? The explanation may lie elsewhere. Men have never been at ease with the solitary God, companionless in eternity. Polytheism was the wrong answer, but to a profoundly right "need." The Trinity is the true answer, but it was not yet known. *Paradise Lost,* which has done so much to color the English-speaking world's picture of the Genesis story, has the Father speaking to the Son. But the plural here is not the Trinity—though one who accepts the Trinity is delighted to find the plural. My own feeling is that "us" might be a kind of unpremeditated, wholly unaware assumption of a companionship within God, which anticipated the revelation of the Trinity—companionship, as it were, breaking in for the making of man! Or it may have been a thrust of the same instinct which produced the plural Elohim for the one God. The Old Testament writers had not the doctrine of the Trinity; but we continually feel them feeling for it.

For the use of "us" a simpler explanation has been offered. The *Jerusalem Bible* thinks it may, and Gerhard von Rad thinks it must, mean that God is discussing man's creation with the angels—God surrounded by his heavenly court as in the sixth chapter of Isaiah, and the first of Job. The word *elohim,* already used for the gods of the pagans before the shattering discovery that Yahweh was Elohim and Elohim Yahweh, continued to be applied to them; and not only to them but to beings less than the one God—to angels, and even to men, judges and rulers, for instance—whose functions were godlike, even if they themselves proved to be considerably less so! Angels are out of fashion today. So learned a Scripture scholar as C. H. Dodd calls them the discarded gods of polytheism. As a theory this would be understandable, but it is stated as if it were the sort of fact that nobody can deny. Even with no revelation from Christ, I should have thought angels just as likely to be what polytheism was feeling for and did not fully reach, since the developed doctrine of angels is so far in advance of polytheism. One hears it said that the Israelites took angels from the Babylonians—the Elohist in particular feeling it did more honor to God to have him in contact with men through angels rather than direct—and that Christ used them because his hearers expected him to. But his phrase "they see the face of my heavenly Father continually" he did not get from Israel or Babylon, neither of which had the doctrine of the Beatific Vision.

The Hymn does not "define" God. It does not define man either. Both are taken as known. But one thing is said about man's making, whose meaning we shall not exhaust until we see God.

... *in our image, after our likeness.* There is nothing like this anywhere else in Scripture. By the Second Commandment images were forbidden, but these were "graven images" made by man, an abiding temptation; while the command was actually being given on Sinai, the Israelites were making an image of the Canaanite god El, worshipped as a bull. And for a thousand years after that the craving was there. So that it was a charged word the writer quotes God as using. In fact it is a direct answer to idolatry. There is but one image of God, man himself, made by the only maker who knew the original! The word "likeness" may be meant to say something not contained in "image." It has been suggested that "likeness" is a way of denying equality, but then so is "image" (outside the Trinity!). If "us" means God and the angels, then "our" does too—we are made in the image of God and the angels: whereas in the next verse we have "God created man in his own image." A similar problem arises with Psalm 8.5: are we made a little less than God or than the angels? There seems to be no point of principle involved—the angels are in any event made in God's image, if we are like God, we are like them: only, of course, as pure spirits their difference from God is less than ours.

The image may in any man be defaced, mutilated. But

that which is defaced, mutilated, is in some sense the portrait
of God, the self-portrait of God. "In some sense"—but in
what sense? Who is like to God? We have just quoted the
Egyptian *Instruction for King Meri-ka-re*—"they who issued from his body are the images." But this was a bodied
image of a bodied god. The Genesis writer could have said
with Isaiah, "horses are flesh, God is spirit" (31.3). We, who
have read Isaiah, concentrate the likeness in man's spirit—
with our finite power to know and love recognized as a
created image of the infinite intellect and will of God.

But the Genesis writer would hardly have thought of God
or men in those terms. Did he think of God as "pure spirit"?
We can answer that as the probabilities strike us: he certainly
did not say it. In any event it is not man's spirit but man
whom God made in his image and likeness, the whole man.
The prime fact about God was his power. When Christ said,
"To God all things are possible," he was saying the one thing
about God that every Jew held: close on sixty times in the
Old Testament, he is called "almighty." Man, made in his
image, has power as God has, limited indeed but *like*. So
God tells him that he is to have dominion "over the animals,"
to "subdue" the earth.

But all the same, intellect and will are basic to likeness.
How would God give dominion over created things to
crocodiles, or convey to lions that they were to subdue the
earth? Man alone knows what is being said. Language is the
key. Power is unusable without the word, in that sense too
man's soul is in his breath.

That God has an uncreated image, the Son eternally be-
gotten, and that the created image must in some way bear
special relation to the uncreated, our writer did not know.

*Male and female he created them. . . . Be fruitful and
multiply.* The writer is clearly thinking of the making not
of a single pair but of the human species. The phrase has

been translated "God created mankind, masculine and feminine." There is no mention here of Adam and Eve, though
he knew the next chapters.

Sex comes into the Hymn with man—the animals had it,
of course, but in them sex was simply for procreation, and
carried no possibility either of glory or degradation: the
mating of animals is not tragic or even comic.

Any pagan might have marvelled that sex made so late an
entry. If one has been reading the myths for too long at a
time, the gods can seem like sexual maniacs. Genesis, of
course, is not simply mythology fumigated; it differs from
end to end. But between the whole of the Old Testament
and the myths one towering difference *is* that there is no sex
activity in God, not a hint of the hierogamy which was
almost de rigueur among the pagans—to each God his
consort! Their primary notion of production was sexual,
either the bodily union of god and goddess (as in one version
of the Marduk story he and the goddess Aruru created the
seed of mankind); or, if no goddess was available, then the
masturbation of the god. Given that sexual union was at the
heart of paganism, the mating of sky and earth was an irresistible reminder, Sky God overlaying Earth Goddess (in this
context the Egyptians are exceptional, as we have noted, in
making Sky female and Earth male). In one Babylonian
myth, Enlil, god of air, was born of their union; in another
he prised them apart (not, one imagines, an early anticipation of the Oedipus complex). Before Mohammed, the Arabs
gave Allah three daughters. The gods did not confine their
adventures in sex to goddesses. The Canaanites had a story
of El, grown old, regaining his virility and delightedly having
intercourse with two women.

For the Jews there was none of this. Not that they were
unaware of sex: it is all over the Old Testament, but where
it belongs—among men and women, not in God. Not for

them was the cry of the Egyptian worshipping Amun—
"Exalted be thy phallus!"

*Fill the earth and subdue it . . . have dominion over every
living thing.* Genesis did not get this from the myths. Scholars
seem to have found no other primitive story that makes man
Lord. Psalm 8 dwells on the idea: "Thou hast given him
dominion over the works of thy hands; thou hast put all
things under his feet."

"Subdue" does not mean "exploit," any more than "dominion" means "tyranny." But exploitation and tyranny are
nearly the whole of man's story. "Subdue the earth"? He has
certainly subdued it. His knife is at its throat. But the earth
has subdued him too, very much as the Greeks subdued—
that is, seduced—their Roman conquerors. The world has
mankind as much in its grip as mankind has the world.

This indeed is a large part of the story that the rest of
Scripture tells. Behind the myths is the war between chaos
and men, chaos and the gods. The war is in Scripture too,
every single episode in it is an episode in that unceasing
war—especially the first episode. But for Scripture there is
to be no twilight of the gods. God is eternal and the issue
is in his hands.

> Thus the heavens and the earth were finished,
> and all the host of them. And in the seventh day
> . . . God rested from all his work which he had
> done in creation.

To the seventh day there is no addition of "evening and
morning." God's rest remains open, all Scripture tells of its
vast energy. For a brief commentary on what God's rest might
mean to us, read Psalm 95.11 and Hebrews 3 and 4.

So the Hymn ends. Of what happens to men it—naturally—
says nothing. Its concern is with Creation. "Thus the heavens

and the earth were finished." It is a hymn, not a narrative. It
was placed there as the Introduction to the Pentateuch, which
has narrative in plenty. With the Hymn completed, we go on
to the Yahwist's centuries-older telling of man's beginnings.
In Chapter 5 the Priest returns to give Adam's begetting of
Seth "in his own likeness, after his own image," and the roll
of Seth's descendants down to Noah and his three sons.

The Hymn of Creation does not tell, or even ask, why God
created at all. Scripture nowhere suggests that God needed
man. It tells why he created woman—because "it is not good
for man to be alone." It does not say, "It is not good for
God to be alone."

Not in so many words.

A THEOLOGICAL POSTSCRIPT

We know more of what is contained in "the heavens and the
earth" than the Priest knew. Of angels he could have known
something, not of electrons at the sub-microscopic end or
the vastness of time and space at the super-telescopic. What
is more important we can, as he could not, read his words
"God created" as "Father, Son and Holy Spirit created." I
shall not try to repeat or summarize what was said of the
Trinity in *God and the Human Mind*. What concerns us
here is the bearing of this deeper knowledge of the Creator
upon our understanding of the act of Creation and its
purpose.

The distinction of action among the Persons is a mystery
of the inner life of God. All the outgoing actions, the actions
upon created being, are the actions of all Three, for the
power by which they act belongs in its totality to each. There
is a faint similarity between Father and Son acting as one
in producing the Holy Spirit, and in the Three acting as

one in producing creatures, sustaining them, and operating in and upon them. Yet the distinction of Persons is not for nothing in divine operations upon created being, any more than in the production of the Third Person within the Godhead. For the Three are not to be thought of as mere facsimiles, a top copy and two carbons. Each is wholly God, but each has his own way of being God; the distinctions are as infinite as the oneness.

We find in Scripture that in certain exterior operations the part of one or other of the Three is given special mention. At the Last Supper, for instance, Christ insists that the Son and the Holy Spirit have a difference of function in relation to men. When the Apostles were desolate that Christ was leaving them, he gave as sufficient reason that, if he did not go, the Holy Spirit would not come (John 16.7). By his very insistence he showed it as in some way essential that the Holy Spirit, that other Paraclete, should come in his place—which means that something would result from the presence of the Third Person that would not come from Christ's. Even if he meant that he was leaving this world only as man, the question remains why he should not as God do whatever it is that he is so insistent must be done by the Third Person (who proceeds from him). The Holy Spirit did come at Pentecost, ten days after our Lord had ascended to his Father; and the whole of the New Testament story of Christ's Church is of the presence and guidance and governance of the Holy Spirit.

How does this relate to the general principle that every operation of the divine Nature upon creatures is the operation of all Three Persons? Observe first that its attribution (the theologians call it appropriation) is not at hazard but follows a pattern—any given work of God among men may be attributed to that one of the Persons whose mode of subsistence within the Trinity it mirrors. Thus, to the Father, who is Origin, Creation is especially attributed; to the Son,

who subsists by the way of knowledge or wisdom, the works
of wisdom; to the Holy Spirit, who subsists by the way of
love, the works of love. We are accustomed to this in regard
to sanctification. Here we glance at it in regard to Creation.
In the Creeds, God the Father is called Creator, and we have
just seen why. But in the opening of John's Gospel the Second Person is shown as concerned in Creation too—"through
him all things were made": and we find this also in the
Epistles, especially in the opening of Hebrews—"through
whom he created the world."

"There is one God the Father *from* whom are all things
and *for* whom we exist, and one Lord, Jesus Christ, through
whom are all things and through whom we exist" (1 Cor.
8.6). The preposition "through" is in the first and second
chapters of Hebrews, Colossians 1.16 has it, with the addition
of "in" and "for."

As we look closely at the problem, we find some beginning
of light. Creation means that something is where nothing
was, that something is brought into existence without the
use of pre-existing material: as such it was a work of sheer
origination and the Father comes first to our mind. But creation is not only that. What is brought by it into existence is
not just any something, but a universe ordered to an ultimate fullness of being: as such it is a work of wisdom and the
part played in it by the Second Person is underlined. More
than that, creation was, in some special way, meant to issue
in man, the created image of God—and the Second Person
was the uncreated image of the Father.

What of the Third Person? We are back at the question
Why God created. We can be certain that creation was not
merely a matter of whim, produced by God to while away
the boredom of eternity. He had a purpose in it. But what?
The myths show the gods creating men as servants, to ease
their own labors. But the God of Israel, "sending his call to

that which is not as if it already were," needed no such service. Our sense that love must have been creation's purpose is shown valid when we find Christ giving as the first of his great commands that we should love God. In the awareness of that, our minds move instinctively to the Holy Spirit, who within the Godhead *is* love.

So we speak of creation, the process and the product, as issuing from the Father, by way of the Son, unto the Spirit who is love; we realize how crude is our effort at utterance, but the crudeness is not lightless. We are saying something. Appropriation is not fiction. It is a concentration upon one of the Persons in an action performed by all Three. But that one really *is* in action: and in action *as himself*. Just as the Three are One God yet distinct, they are one principle of exterior operation yet distinct. There is no pointless repetition in their action any more than in their existence. Each possesses the divine Nature as his own, each possesses it in his own way, each has his own way of operating in it upon creatures.

We have not light enough to proceed far on this line of thought. However we may analyze Creation, it remains one single, simple action of power, wisdom and love performed by Three Persons, each one of whom is Power and Wisdom and Love. Yet it is at least interesting to note that whereas in the making of the order of creation we concentrate especially on the Son's part, its marring brought that same Son into the world incarnate: and the Incarnation is *not* the incarnation of all Three with the Son's part emphasized, it is his solely.

NOTES

1. D: Douay version.
2. *From the Stone Age to Christianity,* p. 17.

3. K: *The Holy Bible,* trans. Ronald Knox. Copyright 1944, 1948 and 1950, Sheed and Ward, Inc. Reprinted with the permission of His Eminence, the Cardinal of Westminster.

4. *Patterns in Comparative Religion,* p. 97.

5. From S. G. F. Brandon, *Creation Legends of the Ancient Near East* (Mystic, Conn.; Lawrence Verry, Inc., 1963).

6. Speiser, *op. cit.*

4

The Beginning of Man

WE HAVE ALREADY NOTED the possibility that the Hymn of
Creation might well have been produced by a deeply spiritual
man, long meditating on the "I am" which God had given
as his name to Moses, with the aid of light and impulse from
God of whose action within him he may have known nothing.
It is equally possible that an earlier man of the same
spirituality, similarly aided by God, might have written
Genesis 2-3. Concentrating all the powers of a mind evidently
rich and powerful upon the contrast between the world
which actually is and any world God could conceivably have
wanted, such a man might have seen that it must have come
through man wanting to be his own God. If so, whose act
would that insight have been, his or God's? It must have
been blinding. Whether or not he knew grace was at work
in him, it is hard to believe that he was not as convinced
as any of the prophets that his message was God's.

The two mysteries on which he sought light were sin and
death. He is answering his own questions, rather like the
Egyptian author of the *Dialogue of a Man with His Own
Soul,* written a thousand years or more earlier. It is perhaps

the earliest criticism of life that has come down to us; certainly nothing of the sort has been found, or is thinkable, in Canaan or even in Mesopotamia. The Egyptian is concerned (like the Yahwist) with life and death. He is urging the case for suicide not because of any great expectation of joy in the world to come, but solely because of the misery of being alive. The poem begins:

> Behold my name stinks
> More than the stench of fish
> On a summer's day
>   When the sky is hot.

Then he goes into detail:

> Brothers are evil
> The companions of yesterday no longer
>   live. . . .
> Hearts are rapacious
> Every man seeks the goods of another. . . .
> One who should make men enraged by his
>   evil behaviour
>   Makes everyone laugh. . . .

> I am laden with misery
> Through lack of an intimate.

Then the praises of death, ending:

> Death is in my sight today
> Like the longing of a man to see home
> ˙When he has spent many years in captivity.

What his Soul answered him after all this could hardly be
meagrer:

> *Put aside care, my comrade and brother . . .*
>   *cling to life—*

Live till you die, in fact. Then

> *Let us make our abode together.*[1]

The Genesis writer is not thus complaining of life. He is
trying to understand it. Why in particular should the living
God create a world in which the highest beings, capable of
knowing him and loving him, must die? Why should the
all-pure God bring into existence beings who find purity
almost impossible to retain? For the profoundly religious
man, which our Egyptian was very much not (he has one
perfunctory reference to the god Re), the coexistence of
either sin or death with God is a mystery: the one thing
he feels in the very roots of his being is that God does not
want them, that some other element must have intervened.

The Yahwist saw death and sin as connected—connected
causally at least, in that death came to men because sin had
first come. Did he see that they are connected in essence too?
Pécher c'est mourir un peu—each sin is a death in miniature,
a denial of the fullness of life, made possible by the fact that
the creature *is* a creature, not infinite, capable of choosing
a lesser good. Was he the first to see this? Certainly there is
in the myths nothing like his concern with the nature and
origin of sin. Did he see it at all? I feel certain that he did.
At any rate he links the coming of death with the commission
of sin. And the essence of the sin he sees as the element in
men upon which he shows the tempter playing, the desire
to be like god.

That insight he felt he must utter. So he tells the story of
Adam and Eve, a man and a woman at the beginning of our
race. He does not report it literally. And there are those who
think that if a narrative is not literally true, it is not true
at all—or at least that whatever truth it has is of the order of
significance, not the order of event. But this story does belong
to the order of event. The writer had to cast it into figurative
form because that was the one way in which he could tell it,
given that he was certain only of the basic structure of what
must have happened, and had no knowledge whatever of
the details of its happening.

In the surrounding paganisms (as in many of which the
Jews as yet knew nothing) there were ingenious stories about
the mode of man's making, about woman issuing from man,
about a tree of life. And Mesopotamia had stories in plenty
about the longing for immortality—gained by Utnapishtim;
snatched from Gilgamesh, who at the last shrank away from
death, lamenting: offered by the high god to Adapa and re-
fused by him (he not knowing what was being offered) under
the counselling of the god Ea whom he thought his friend.
Adapa is sometimes spoken of as an earlier Adam: apart
from the first three letters of their names, there seems to
me no resemblance whatever. Certainly there is no hint,
either in the Adapa story or in any of the others, of what I
have called the insight, the basic structure, which was the
Yahwist's whole concern. As to the details, he made his own
selection among the vast profusion the myths supplied—made
his own selection, somewhat as Shakespeare took the framework of the story of Hamlet from Saxo Grammaticus, and
produced a work as original as Shakespeare's, with an immeasurably more powerful hold upon the minds of men.

Pause upon the originality. When he comes to Abraham,
the Yahwist is dealing with historical times and living traditions. He cannot do as he pleases with what has come down

to him, cannot mutilate or invent—though he can see new
significances. But of the creation of man there was no history,
no living traditions. He could do his own thinking and praying, and could write his own certainty in his own way. We
should be on our guard against a tendency to trace everything in these two chapters to an earlier source—myth or
legend or romance—and, when none such is discoverable, to
assume a tradition now lost. No one would dream of applying such a treatment to *Hamlet*. With great writers we allow
for inspiration; even if one did not believe the Yahwist inspired by God, it would be hard to deny him inspiration as
we use the word of great artistic achievement.

How then are these chapters to be classified? As a parable,
like the Good Samaritan? As an extended parable, as Jonah
and his whale may be, or Daniel and his lions? Parables tell
universal truths in the framework of a story invented to
convey them. Their whole point lies in their meaning: nothing would be added to that by the discovery that a particular Jew was in fact vomited up by a whale whose skeleton
has been identified, another rescued by a given Samaritan.
But the Yahwist is trying to account for an existing situation
—the reign of sin and death: unless in essence things happened as he tells them, nothing is accounted for.

The Egyptian myths, we have noted, were not much concerned with man, their interest was in the gods. There is a
papyrus of round the time of Moses, for instance, which says,
"Then man came into being," without a word as to how.
We have seen the god Khepri shedding tears which turned
into men and women; and we have the same idea in the
story of a lotus transformed into the figure of a boy from
whose tears mankind were made. But in general the Egyptians seem not to have thought either man's origin or nature
of sufficient importance to call for lingering.

For the Babylonians, from whom Abraham came and with

whom the Jews had been more recently in contact, it was different. We have already glanced at the creation of men by the god Marduk. It is worth a longer glance. He says:

> "Blood will I mass and cause bones to be.
> I will establish a savage, man shall be his name."[2]

But his father, Ea, the Sumerian Enki, suggested a more interesting plan—that one of the rebel gods should be slain and man made of his blood. And so it was done, Kingu being the god chosen. With this we come close to a very early Hindu story, in which the other gods carve up Purusha, with priests made from his mouth, soldiers from his arms, farmers from his thighs. And the Chinese have a story of Pan Ku dying and being carved up, his lice becoming the first men—suggesting a scorn for the human race which would have pleased Dean Swift.

To return to Babylon. In the half-millennium between the Marduk story and Genesis, there were variations on the legend—Marduk and his sister Aruru together producing the seed of mankind; Ea himself creating man; the same Ea giving the general idea and leaving other gods to carry it out. A late story has two gods slain, with the reason for producing men stated: "The service of the gods is to be their portion." Some of the variations were added, one feels, for the fun of it.

Behind the story of mankind made from the dismembered Kingu lie two reasons—Kingu was wicked, so that sin and death were in man's very constitution; he was a god, which accounts for man's superiority in intelligence to the rest of creatures.

All this embroidery Genesis ignores.

> The Lord God formed man of dust from the ground . . .

We have already noted that God is called Yahweh Elohim in these chapters (only once outside them, that perhaps by a copyist's slip). My own guess is that the Compiler added Elohim here at the beginning, to make clear that the Yahweh of the next chapters is the Elohim of the Hymn of Creation.

One hears it said that Genesis 1 and Genesis 2 give contradictory accounts of creation. But they do not. They are talking of two different matters—Genesis 1 of the Creation of the Universe, Genesis 2 of the making of man. Speiser sees the difference of topic in the reversal of order—"the heavens and the earth" of Genesis 1, "the earth and the heavens" of Genesis 2. Upon the origin of man each makes a statement—Genesis 2 upon what man is made *of*, the dust of the earth, Genesis 1 on what man is made *like*.

In what we may call the framework, they differ as to the "when" of man's making. The Hymn places it on the sixth day, after the animals, Genesis 2 before vegetation, which the Hymn has on the third day.

The writer may have had in mind a Sumerian myth of the Deluge which says that after the gods fashioned man

Vegetation luxuriated from the earth
Animals were brought artfully into existence.[3]

In any event the Yahwist does not relate creation to the days of the Hebrew week—he is not writing a hymn. Nor is he writing a chronicle. Each writer, in fact, has his own way of symbolizing man's superiority to the animals.

The forming of man of dust from the ground has been seen as being the image of a potter making his pottery—the verb used, *yasar,* is the potter's verb. There were plenty of instances in the myths. The Mesopotamian goddess Manu is pictured as making man out of handfuls of clay. In the Gilgamesh epic, Enkidu's father was created of clay by Aruru.

There is a famous bas-relief at Luxor, dated probably round 1400 B.C., in which the ram-headed god Khnum is fashioning an infant pharaoh (and his Ka, a kind of astral body) on a potter's wheel. This was, of course, not the creation of the first man; but the connection of ideas is obvious. In any event, if one is to have any picture at all for the shaping of man, the one maker of a shaped object known to everybody was precisely the potter.

The image recurs in both Testaments. Isaiah could say to God, "We are the clay and you are the potter" (64.8). And it is almost a verbal quotation of Isaiah (45.9 and 29.16) that we find St. Paul giving the Romans: "Will what is moulded say to its moulder 'Why have you made me thus?' Has the potter no right over the clay, to make out of the same lump one vessel for beauty and one for menial use?" (Rom. 9.20 f.).

Yet it is not certain that the image of the potter is what the Genesis author had chiefly in mind. The word he used is not "clay" but "earth" or "soil," and this seems to be not a mere verbal chance. He uses the word *adamah* which means earth and which gives a reason for calling the first man Adam; Adam was dust and was to return to the dust, was to till the earth of which he was made, was to multiply and fill the earth. "Clay" would not have fitted any of these. And the symbolism of earth and clay is different. "Clay" suggests the potter and his wheel, and to that extent ends in itself; it figures the mode of the making but tells nothing of the being that is made. "Earth" emphasizes man's kinship with all that is. "All men are from the ground and Adam was created of the dust" (Sir. 33.10). Though made in God's image and likeness, man is not a stranger imposed upon the universe from outside. It is very much as Christ, though he is the only-begotten son of God, is not outside humanity but belongs fully in it.

> . . . and breathed into his nostrils the breath of
> life and man became a living soul.

The writers of Genesis do not say what their idea of God
is; their minds seem not to have worked that way, their
whole concentration is upon what God wants of men and
can do for them. Nor do they say what man is, they assume
that their readers know a man when they see one. But at
least they tell enough of the mode of man's production to
show something of what they think the finished product is.
Or do they? Made *of* earth, and made *in the image* of God,
but made into what?

The reader brought up on the ordinary Christian view of
man as a union of spirit and matter, spirit embodied or body
enspirited, might misread the words "God breathed into his
nostrils the breath of life and man became a living soul."
The writer did not mean that man was given a spiritual soul,
distinguishing him from the animals. A dozen verses later
the animals too are spoken of as "living souls." The phrase
simply means "living beings."[4] For a spiritual soul we must·
wait a good many centuries till a Jew, trained in Greek philosophy and writing in Greek, could speak of God as "the one
who formed man and inspired him with an active soul and
breathed into him a living spirit" (Wis. 15.11). For the
ultimate fullness of meaning that the Genesis word "breathes"
could carry, we must wait a further couple of centuries till
the first Easter Sunday, when the God-man breathed upon
the Apostles and said, "Receive ye the Holy Spirit."

That there was a real distinction in man's actions between
bodily and spiritual, these early Jews could not fail to realize:
they could express the difference with words like "body"
and "flesh" and "spirit." But they did not see these as constituent elements within man. Man is simply man. "My
spirit," "my soul" and "my flesh" were all ways of saying "I."

Animation by God's breathing into man is only in Genesis, the myths know nothing of it. The Egyptian *Instruction for King Meri-ka-re,* with its "God made the breath for their nostrils," comes nearest, but how far that nearest is. For the Jews, who did not think (as the writer of the *Instruction* did) that man issued from the body of God, and who dismissed the phallic activity of the Gentile gods without even the compliment of uttered denial, breathing was the aptest figure for the communication of life.

God took earth, shaped it, breathed upon it, and man was alive. The formation and the animation are stated as two distinct steps—somewhat as in the Luxor bas-relief the god Khnum shapes the infant Pharaoh, while the goddess Hathor holds out the symbol of life. For the Jew, the same breath of God which brought man into existence maintained him in it: when it was withdrawn, he died. Thus Elihu reminds Job (34.14, K), "God has but to turn his thoughts towards men, reclaiming the spirit he once breathed into them, and all life would fail everywhere, mankind would return to its dust." And this was the pattern of life and death for animals too—"when thou takest away thy breath, they die and return to their dust" (Ps. 104.29).

I have had to devote a great deal of space to what the Genesis writer is telling us. He himself is content to say that God made man and made him alive. Later Jewish commentators could let themselves go. The one who described Adam as stretched from one end of the earth to the other, his head level with the divine throne, was saying something profound. The one who said that compared with God Adam was an ape, compared with Adam Eve was an ape, was saying something not very profound but intensely felt. The one who made Adam seventy feet high was betraying the poverty of his imagination.

THE BEGINNING OF MAN

> And the Lord God planted a garden in Eden, in
> the East; and there he put the man whom he had
> formed.

The Sumerians had had a paradisal place, Dilmun, watered
from below as Genesis says the earth was before God formed
man. But it was for the gods, and for the occasional human
who became a god—Utnapishtim of the *Epic of Gilgamesh*
was one. Apart from Dilmun, there are gardens in plenty in
the myths, but Genesis is unique in showing the human race
as beginning in one. "Eden" may be from the Sumerian
word, *edinu,* meaning a plain or a steppe: the Septuagint
translates it as *paradeisos,* from a Persian word meaning a
park fenced round. Eden remained deep in the Jewish mind.
Other peoples had some sort of paradisal state at the beginning, but the Jews looked for its return. "The Lord will
comfort Zion . . . and will make her wilderness like Eden,
her desert like the garden of the Lord" (Is. 51.3).

It is hard not to feel that this ancestral concept took possession of that otherwise sober sociologist Karl Marx, with
his picture of the Classless Society and his certainty that it
must come. However that may be, it was in the mind of
Christ in agony when he said to the repentant sinner agonizing on the next cross, "This day you shall be with me in
paradise."

Observe that Genesis wastes no time on the framework.
Isaiah could elaborate on Eden restored—"The wolf shall
dwell with the lamb, the leopard shall lie down with the
kid, and the lion shall eat straw like the ox. And a little
child shall lead them. The suckling child shall play over the
asp's hole, the weaned child shall put his hand in the adder's
den" (Is. 11.6-9). And later writers, outside Scripture, could
let their imagination have a carnival on the same theme—

apples of gold, grapes as big as melons—all that sort of thing.
Our writer spares us this. He does not know the detail of
man's beginning, and sees no point in inventing. He knows
the garden is a metaphor and he sketches it in a dozen words
—"every tree that is pleasant to the sight and good to eat."
With the same sparseness of detail he carries the metaphor
forward with mention of two other trees, differently fruitful
—the tree of life symbolizing the possibility of immortality;
and the tree of the knowledge of good and evil symbolizing
the possibility of sin and death. Sin and death, good and
evil are his real theme.

Next comes the forming by God of beasts and birds, and
their naming by men. Pause for a moment on this. Unbelievers make fun of it, with animals in their myriads parading
before man and being allotted a name (how, says a ques-
tioner, did they get the duck-billed platypus to leave his
solitude?). Believers solemnly explain that it was only the
birds and animals of Eden that Adam named, which made
the numbers manageable (and excluded the duck-billed
platypus). Our very sophisticated writer would have laughed
at both, especially the second. Given the vast importance
attached by his world to the "name," he was simply saying
what the writer of the Hymn of Creation was to express
when he said that man was given dominion over the rest of
creatures. Their inferiority to man was the sole point of the
story: for a companion man needed one of his own kind.
So...

> So the Lord God caused a deep sleep to fall upon
> the man, and while he slept took one of his ribs
> . . . and the rib he made into a woman and
> brought her to the man.

There is a whole theology of marriage in the three verses
18-20 compressed in that word "So." "It is not good," God

said, "for man to be alone. I will make him a companion of his own kind." It is a unique reason for bringing woman into existence. One might have thought the continuance of the human race (which Genesis 1 was to emphasize) reason in plenty, but our writer sees companionship as the need women must fill for man; the need, in fact, each must fill for the other. Nearly a thousand years later the writer of Wisdom, remembering this chapter, could write "In the womb of a mother I was moulded into flesh . . . from the seed of a man and *the pleasure of marriage.*"

The making of woman, like the making of man, is given as a completion that was needed: man completes earth's incompleteness, woman completes man's. The parallel is interesting:

> The earth was barren ("with no one to till it")
> man was made from earth
> he was called Adam (from adamah, earth)
>
> Man was alone ("not good for him . . .")
> woman was made from man
> she was called Ishshah (from *ish,* man)

Did the Yahwist know the completion humanity itself needed and would one day receive—man made from earth, woman from man, Christ from woman? How much he actually knew *we* cannot know. God may have revealed more than is written. In any event, he may have anticipated much. It seems to me that Genesis is messianic from end to end: but then, I believe in the Messiah!

How woman, so like, so different, was to be accounted for occupied the minds not only of the Jews but of all races. In myths as far away as Australia and the Pacific Ocean, in philosophy as profound as Plato's and religions as subtle as Gnosticism, in some of the rabbinic writers, we find the notion that man began bi-sexual, androgynous, with a variety of theories as to how the division happened. Mircea Eliade quotes *Bereshith rabbah*: "Adam and Eve were made back to back, attached at their shoulders; then God separated them with an axe, or cut them in two. Others have a different picture; the first man, Adam, was a man on his right side, a woman on his left; but God split him into two halves."[5]

Our writer did not pretend that he knew how woman was formed—Luther's great opponent, the Dominican Cardinal Cajetan, thought the account he gave was to be taken as simply a parable. But a parable carefully thought out. Neither the "deep sleep," for instance, nor the "rib" is there by chance!

The sleep, *tardemah*, is not ordinary sleep. The Septuagint translates it as "ecstasy." We find the same Hebrew word before the covenant with Yahweh; "A deep sleep fell on Abraham and a dread and a great darkness" (Gen. 15.12).

"Rib" is only a guess: the exact meaning of *tsela* is not known with certainty. That the Yahwist was thinking of the Sumerian goddess Nin-ti, which means "lady of the rib," seems improbable; his readers would hardly have noticed that in Sumerian there was a kind of pun involved, between the word "rib" and the word "life"! But "rib" does lead admirably into the insight he puts into the mouth of Adam—

> "This at last is bone of my bones, and flesh of
> my flesh; she shall be called Woman (ishshah)
> because she was taken out of Man (ish)."

This is the point of the parable, if parable it is; it is what the whole episode is building towards.

A word as to Eve's name. *Ishshah* is not connected etymologically with *ish* in Hebrew. The Jews tended to link words by their sound rather than by their meaning, precisely be-

cause for them the sound was itself a thing of power, not as
for us only an indicating noise. Woman, of course, was not
her name. Scholars have found names which strike them as
like Eve. There was Heba, wife of a Hittite god, at some
period worshipped in Jerusalem; and the Greeks had Hebe,
who married Herakles. Neither name strikes us as very close
to Hawwah, which Genesis tells us Adam called her—after
the Fall!—because she was, or was to be, "the mother of all
the living." The etymology here is better than with *ishshah*,
the word *hawwah* being sufficiently close to the Hebrew for
life, living.

> Therefore a man leaves his father and his mother
> and cleaves to his wife. And they become one
> flesh.

Some scholars think these words are there because long ago
land inheritance was through the female line, so that a man
would be wise to stay with his wife. One feels such scholars
must be tone-deaf. From that tone-deafness Christ did not
suffer; he quotes those words and carries them further—
"Therefore what God has joined, let not man put asunder."
Nor does it affect Paul, who sees them as making the union
of wife and husband a symbol of the union of Christ and
his Church (Eph. 5.31).

These sentences are a complete assertion both of woman's
fundamental equality with man and of the unbreakableness
of marriage. How much of what they contain is offered us
as said by Adam, who had no father or mother to leave? How
much as comment by the writer? And had he any suspicion
of the truth, uttered by Christ, that they were God's? They
express what God meant marriage to be, of course, rather
than what man has made of it: just as Psalm 8—"You have
made him little less than the angels, and crown him with

glory and honor"—expresses what God meant man to be, rather than what man has made of himself. Whether man or marriage has fallen further from what God wanted is anybody's guess.

When did the writer think all this happened? The mistake made by men who thought that a date for the creation of the universe could be extracted from the life-schedules of the Patriarchs, we have already looked at. Here we may glance at the making of man. Our ancestors had no reason to think of this as a process spread over thousands of years, moving forward by stages. Therefore they assumed it was instantaneous—so, probably, did the Genesis writer, if he gave it any thought at all. Modern geology has given us reason to think it was thus spread: and most of us do assume a long stretch of time and many stages—Evolution, in fact. The word "formed" can fit either instantaneous or progressive production. (I don't mean that the Yahwist was inspired to choose that word because it could leave room for what the scientists might one day discover!)

No specifically religious questions seem to be involved. Whether God formed man's body in one act or by an unfolding process, God is still at our origin. We may, if we see it so, hold that there was a development from one animal body to another till one emerged which was capable of union with a spiritual soul and God saw to it that the union should be. Whatever the process, man had appeared on our planet. The drama could begin.

NOTES

1. T. W. Thacker's translation in D. Winston-Thomas, ed., *Documents from Old Testament Times* (New York, Nelson, 1965).

2. Speiser, *op. cit.*

3. Quoted in Mircea Eliade, *From the Primitives to Zen* (New York, Harper, 1966).

4. This is how the *Revised Standard Version* translates it: but the Hebrew word is "soul."

5. *Patterns in Comparative Religion*, p. 423.

5

The Beginning of Sin

It has taken us a long time to unwrap what Genesis tells of the making of man and woman and of their world as they first knew it; but the writer himself wasted no time on either. On the condition of man thus fresh from the hand of God he is as economical.

Milton could describe "our general sire":

> *His fair large front and eye sublime declared*
> *Absolute rule; and hyacinthine locks*
> *Round from his parted forelock manly hung*
> *Clustering, but not beneath his shoulders broad.*

The Yahwist pretended to no such very detailed knowledge, nor would he have seen any point in inventing. But of the essentials he feels sure.

In their beginning the first man and woman were at one with God; although the author's mention of God's "walking in the garden in the cool of the day" comes after they had

91

sinned, the impression it gives is of something habitual
which their sin was to bring to an end: one feels that the
phrase conveys the author's personality, genius, un-need of
tradition; certainly no phrase could convey more livingly the
reality of close communion with God.

And they were at one with themselves and each other. One
detail suffices to convey this—"they were naked and not
ashamed": it suffices because it shows the most turbulent of
human powers completely under control: the sexual powers
were man's, not he theirs. Powers out of control mean cor-
ruption in man's being. So the writer of Wisdom sees it: God
made man for "incorruption" (2.23). He goes further—"God
made him in the image of God's own eternity, but through
the devil's envy death entered the world." A chapter earlier,
Wisdom had said, "God did not make death . . . he created
all things that they might exist, and the generative forces of
the world are wholesome, and there is no destructive power
in them" (1.13 f.). Is freedom from death also in God's plan
as Genesis states it?

This brings us to the two trees. The Genesis writer did not
need to think those up for himself—the Babylonians had at
the eastern entry of heaven two trees, of Truth and of Life.
These fitted precisely what he had to utter, though he found
a name for the first of them which suited his purpose more
precisely still—tree of the Knowledge of Good and Evil: that
name was wholly his.

The other, the tree of Life, was a standard item in the
mythologies. For men of all religions—for those men of the
Near East as for the Scandinavians, the Druids in Gaul and
Britain, Australia's aborigines—trees signified nature's cease-
less power to renew herself. The idea of a tree as a channel
or principle of life at the center of the universe—as this one
"in the midst of the garden"—is to be found all over the

world. To the Western peoples the best known is the one
in the Scandinavian *Volüspa*—"The tree set up in wisdom
which grows down to the bosom of the earth." Our writer
naturally had no advance knowledge of what Scandinavians
would one day hold. But he knew the Sumerian *Epic of
Gilgamesh* (the name means "he who experienced all"),
which is concerned with the hero's search for a tree or herb
that will make him immortal—knew it and adapted it to
his own use.

There is a general impression that the *Gilgamesh* poem
is at the root of, or at least profoundly influenced, the Adam
and Eve story, and also the Genesis account of the Flood. It
is worth dwelling on:

The hero, Gilgamesh, part divine, is of unbridled arrogance,
raping and killing. As a way of bringing him under control,
the goddess Aruru conceived within her a double of the
high god Anu—"pinched off the clay and cast it on the
steppe": copulated with it and produced Enkidu—a primitive man, naked but for his hairiness, living only with wild
animals: he maddens hunters by saving animals from their
"pits and snares." So they send a temple prostitute to
seduce him out of the wilderness into the city, where Gilgamesh can dispose of him. For a week he enjoys her "ripe-
ness," then returns to his animals, but they now flee from
him. The girl persuades him to come with her to Uruk.
He and Gilgamesh fight, as the hunters hoped, but become
friends: together they slay a bull sent to slay Gilgamesh
(because, having been seduced by the goddess Ishtar, he
refuses to marry her, reminding her of the lovers she has
betrayed). Enkidu dies, at first cursing the temple harlot,
then turning his curses into blessings—may old men and
young alike find her irresistible. Gilgamesh is shattered by
his friend's death:

"When I die, shall I too not be like Enkidu?
Woe has entered my belly."[1]

So he sets out in pursuit of immortality. At last he gets to Utnapishtim, survivor of the great Flood, the story of which he relates. He warns Gilgamesh of the inevitability of death, but tells him of a plant which will give him, not immortality, but at least revival of youth. After many adventures he finds the plant, and starts back to Uruk with it. On the way he eats a morsel, then bathes. While he is bathing "a serpent sniffs the fragrance of the plant," comes up and carries it off. So when death comes to Gilgamesh, he can only meet it lamenting.

The epic as a whole is at the opposite pole from the story told in Genesis: indeed it is unthinkable in any part of Scripture. What have the two in common? The animals?—perhaps; the temptation of Enkidu?—apart from a certain common element in all temptations, these two have just about no resemblance; the serpent? not a tempter, just a snake who wanted the fragrance for himself and stole the plant; the plant of immortality? But Adam was not seeking immortality or tempted by its promise; the tree of Life does not figure in the Genesis story. There is no Fall—Gilgamesh was a horror to begin with, he could hardly have got worse. Once or twice a detail comes closer, as we shall see, but always with a wholly non-Gilgamesh meaning.

> The Lord God commanded the man, saying,
> "You may freely eat of every tree of the garden,
> but of the tree of the knowledge of good and evil
> you shall not eat, for in the day you eat of it
> you shall die."

Given the universality of the sacred tree in the religions the Jews knew best, it is of interest that the tree of Life is men-

tioned only to vanish from the story. We have to wait for
the last book of the New Testament to meet it again—in the
heavenly Jerusalem: "In the midst of the street of the City,
and on either side of the river, was the tree of Life . . . and
the leaves of the tree were for the healing of the nations."
(Apoc. 22.2) Does his mention of it in the Garden mean that
the Yahwist saw man as meant by God to escape death? The
penalty God attaches to the eating of the other tree suggests
it. If so, its vanishing is sufficiently accounted for—*Adam did
sin,* and the tree of life was not for him. It must await the
coming of one who conquers where Adam failed—"to him I
will grant to eat of the tree of life which is in the Paradise
of God" (Apoc. 2.7).

Much humor has been lavished on the fruit the man was
forbidden to eat. There have been plenty of guesses as to the
tree—date, olive, grapevine (favored in the *Mishna*): apple
is traditional in the Western world. Genesis, of course, does
not speak of an apple—the word is fruit, fruit of the tree of
the Knowledge of Good and Evil. The writer might have
smiled at efforts to decide the tree, as over the rabbinic discussion of the length of time (varying from six hours to seven
years) Adam and Eve refrained from eating the forbidden
fruit. His phrase has metaphor written all over it. The trees
that grow in gardens are not like that.

Why, we may wonder, did he change the name of this one
tree—the Babylonians called it tree of Truth? What did "the
knowledge of good and evil" mean to him? It may have been
one of those pairs of opposites—like heaven and earth; a way
of saying "everything." We have Absalom speaking "neither
good nor bad"—i.e., not speaking at all—to Amnon (2 Sam.
13.22). And in *Peake's Commentary,* S. H. Hooke speaks of
myths known to the Yahwist in which the words were used
of "the secret things belonging to God, the knowledge of
powerful spells and incantations"—magic, in fact, which was

as such forbidden to the Jews. But later uses in the Old Testament would not bear either meaning. To David, for instance, the woman of Tekoa says: "My lord the king is like the angel of God to discern good and evil" (2 Sam. 14.17): when Sirach summarizes the Genesis story of "man's creation out of earth," we are told that "God showed them both good and evil" (17.6). In other words, the discernment of good and evil, arrived at by living life in union with God's law, is wholly good. The sin lies in making one's own decisions of good and evil without reference to God's command.

In English as in Hebrew phrases can be used to convey a total meaning without advertence to their individual words —we can speak of "Dutch courage" without the faintest thought of Holland, of selling a business "lock, stock and barrel" without thinking of a gun. Whatever "knowledge of good and evil" might mean as a whole phrase, the Yahwist was quite capable of noticing its individual words. Considering his concern with the presence of *evil* in a world made *good* by God, he would hardly have missed the aptness of these two words to his theme.

Seen thus, the name of the tree embodied the consequence of every sin men have ever committed, but most catastrophically the consequence of the first sin: the sinner would come to have a special kind of knowledge of good and evil. Already he knew what "good" meant, but there are elements in good that are to be known most piercingly only in its loss. Already he knew what "evil" meant as an idea, now he would get the bleak knowledge which came from experiencing it in his own self. In Christ himself we find a similar passage to new knowledge by the way of experience. He knew all about obedience, yet "He learned obedience by the things he suffered" (Heb. 5.8). The first sinner learnt disobedience by disobeying, and the suffering has never ceased.

II

Now the serpent was more subtle than any other
wild creature God had made. He said to the
woman. . . .

So begins one of the best-known stories in the world. By
what happened the human race is affected in its very depth,
not one of us is not concerned in it. The Yahwist gives it six
· verses, under two hundred words. There is no known tradition behind it; and oddly enough it did not itself become a
tradition, it is barely referred to again in the Old Testament.
Libraries have been written on it.

The first sin is shown not as originating in man but as
suggested to him. There is no great problem for us in seeing
why there should be a tempter; but we may entertain ourselves wondering why the writer chose to present the tempter
as a serpent. In all the legends coming from Mesopotamia
and the countries round about, the serpent never figures as
a tempter: this does seem to be the Genesis writer's own
contribution. It may be that, since he was telling the story
as happening in a garden, it struck him that nothing—nothing, that is, likely to be found in a garden—would spoil its
pleasure as much as a snake. If so, he must have smiled at
the realization that to cast a serpent for the role of prime
principle of evil would shock millions of serpent worshippers
(including those Israelites who frequented Canaanite sex
rituals) much as his not-yet-born co-author's downgrading of
the Sun in the first chapter would shock the Egyptians and
millions besides. All over the East there was a serpent cult.
To take two of the gods we have met in these pages—Bab-

ylon's Ea was often pictured with a serpent's head, Egypt's Atum (in one story) was to become a serpent at the end, when all else had gone out of existence. In Canaan, a serpent was the symbol of the healing god; his healing implement was a rod with a serpent turned round it.

Serpents did figure in myth and legend, often as dragons (a dragon being a serpent which had eaten another serpent!). They did not act as tempters, but as defenders of things or places which were especially sacred or gave powers beyond the human measure. Before attaining the goal, the hero had to prove himself by overcoming a serpent. In the *Epic of Gilgamesh,* the hero had actually secured the "thorny herb" which would give him length of life, and a serpent stole it from him apparently for its own delectation; there is no moral involved, no conflict, no temptation—Gilgamesh suffers for his carelessness, but Adam for his sin.

The serpent's role in Genesis is quite other, and, as has been noted, without parallel. Did the Genesis writer see the serpent as Satan? What indeed did he know of Satan, or indeed of angels? He ends the story with "cherubim" guarding Eden against human entry, but what did he think they were? It is not unlikely that he had in mind the winged bulls and the twisted swords (symbolizing lightning and thunderbolt) placed at the palace entry in Babylon. Cherub had not yet come to mean angel.

Satan—the word means "opponent"—we meet in the book of Job, where he appears at two meetings of the heavenly court, determined to cause Job to curse God. For this he has to get permission from God, with whom he appears to be at least on negotiating terms. But, that detail apart, he is already shown as vicious enough, determined enough on Job's destruction, to fit Peter's description of the devil as "a beast of prey," "seeking whom he may devour." The whole point of his warfare against men is to get them to curse God. Only

one unfamiliar with the theological view of Satan would
think his having to ask God's permission meant that he was
still an angel in good standing. A theological treatise would
have analyzed Satan's hostility with more particularity; but
he seems to be all there in Job. He does not in our modern
sense "tempt" Job, he only tests him. His first appearance in
the role of tempter, as we use the word today, is when he
incites David, against God's will, to take a census of his
people (1 Chron. 21.1). But Satan may there stand for one
of the gods: Milcom has been suggested.

To return to the serpent. The Old Testament is not much
concerned with Adam and the Fall. It gives us one light only
on our present question. In the Greek-language book of
Wisdom we read "God made man incorruptible, made him
in the image of his own likeness. But by the envy of the
devil, death came into the world" (2.24). In Apocalypse
(12.9) we get the serpent as Satan, not at man's beginning
but near the world's end—"the great dragon was thrown
down, that ancient serpent, who is called the Devil and Satan,
the deceiver of the whole world."

The connection is not made in Genesis. All we can say is
that the writer did not think Adam and Eve were tempted
by a snake; it was not a snake's subtlety he rates so high,
those who have much to do with snakes think them half-
witted. At every point of the story the serpent is clearly a
personal force of evil, enemy of God, enemy of man.

> Did God say, "You shall not eat of any tree of
> the garden"? And the woman said to the serpent,
> "We may eat of the fruit of the trees of the
> garden; but God said, 'You shall not eat of the
> fruit of the tree which is in the midst of the
> garden, neither shall you touch it, lest you die.' "
> But the serpent said to the woman, "You will
> not die. For God knows that when you eat of it

your eyes will be opened, and you will be like
God, knowing good and evil."

So when the woman saw that the tree was good
for food, and that it was a delight to the eyes,
and that the tree was to be desired to make one
wise, she took of its fruit and ate. And she also
gave some to her husband, and he ate.

The serpent begins by misquoting; the devil did the same
in the second temptation of Christ in the desert. Urging that
he hurl himself from the pinnacle of the Temple in the
certainty that the angels will bear him up, he quotes Psalm
91. But the Psalm is speaking of the support God will have
his angels give men as they walk the road of life, not to men
who challenge God to work miracles for their glorification.

His assertion "You will not die if you ignore the command" is wholly modern. The moral law is only a taboo;
life beckons. For the rest, we are here given a blueprint of
every temptation men have ever yielded to—always the same
three stages. The forbidden action is seen as alluring; the
experience will be enriching; to refuse it would be to deny
one's own maturity.

What was the action forbidden by God?

Martin Luther was neither the first nor the last to assume
that the sin to which the serpent tempted Adam and Eve
was sexual intercourse. An early Jewish commentator thought
that Eve and the serpent (who was actually the fiend Samael)
had intercourse then and there, and that Cain was born of
their union. Serpents were, in many places still are, seen as
sex symbols. In the Phrygian mysteries women ritually married the god by sliding snakes—live snakes or images in gold
or ivory—between breasts and thighs.

Luther could not have known that godlikeness, promised
by the serpent to the woman as a reason why she and her

husband should yield to his tempting, is described in the *Epic of Gilgamesh* as the man's condition *after* he had yielded—and the temptation to which he had yielded was the sex act. The temple harlot, having seduced Enkidu, said to him, "Now you are like a god" (and the act has indeed been known to produce precisely that illusion—for about ten minutes). From this distance of time it looks as if the Genesis writer had been struck by the *Gilgamesh* phrase, and seen it as going to the very essence of sin. It is hard not to feel that the writer had in mind to take the genuine insight of the epic, and at once cleanse it and thrust it deeper.

We find the same phrase used by Isaiah (14.12-15) about the King of Babylon—with the added curiosity that he is addressed as Lucifer, which has become a name for Satan. The king is to be "brought down to Sheol, to the depth of the Pit." What was his crime? He had said in his heart—"I will make myself like the most high." Ezekiel (28.8) has much the same condemnation of the Prince of Tyre. He too will be "thrust down into the Pit" because he had said, "I am a god." It is the formula by which the serpent tempted Adam and Eve. It is the central formula of all sin. In Ezekiel God calls it Pride.

We have noted that there have always been some who hold that the first sin was of sexual intercourse and that, but for the Fall, men would have generated unsexually. St. Augustine called this nonsense, and it is hard to make sense of it in the context. The first pair were new-made by God, sex mechanisms and all, and these could hardly have been meant for abstinence. But sex is by no means for nothing in the story as a whole. That the original man should have a wife is natural enough: that the tempter should seduce her first and leave her to work upon her husband will seem natural or not according to one's experience of women. But the first piece of new "knowledge of good and evil" recorded

after their partaking of the tree of Knowledge rather takes
one's breath away—"Then the eyes of both were opened,
and they knew that they were naked; and they sewed fig
leaves together" as a covering (odd that this does not seem
to have led everyone to the conclusion that the forbidden
tree was a fig tree). Their eyes were opened: opened to what?
To themselves, to unsuspected possibilities in themselves, in
fact to the drearier consequences of autonomy. Everyone
knows this opening of the eyes by the commission of a sin of
which he had thought himself incapable: we call it maturity!
We are not supposed to believe that until that moment it had
escaped their notice that they were undressed—"they were
naked and were not ashamed." Sex had been under control,
it never was to be under control again.

One way or other their sin had been Pride: "Pride is the
beginning of all sin" (Sir. 10.15). It opened the way to all the
sins, and the first to arrive was lust. With a writer as skilled
as the man who wrote the story as we now have it, nothing
is by chance. At every moment he knew what he was doing.
It seems clear that he saw what had gone wrong with sex and
marriage as being at the center of what was wrong with the
whole world. That surely is why at the creation of Eve we
are given so superb a statement of the nature of marriage—
"a man leaves his father and his mother and cleaves to his
wife, and they become one flesh."

This primacy of divorceless monogamy cannot be matched
anywhere else in the Old Testament. We must wait until we
hear Christ himself quoting these very words and continuing
"what therefore God has joined together, let no man put
asunder." And we must wait for Paul, the closest of readers
of the beginning of Genesis, to work out for us in more detail, in many places but especially in Romans and 1 Corinthians, the evil state that man is in because of the evil state

sex is in. As we have noted, Paul quotes these words of
Genesis and goes on to show the marriage union as a symbol
of the union of Christ and his Church.

To summarize: the one thing Genesis tells us of the sin is
that it was an action of disobedience to God. There is no
great point in speculating as to what the action was. The
writer did not know; or regard it as important to know. He
was not thinking in those terms. He was concerned with the
choice of what one wants as against what God wants, the
thrust of man's will against God's. And he certainly saw that
the command here, as with all God's commands in the moral
order, is a statement of the reality of things—*this* will have
as certain consequence *that*.

Yet the very fact of the command means that man is free
to choose. In Sirach's great phrase, "Before a man are life
and death, good and evil; whichever he chooses will be given
to him" (15.18). The tree of which they were not to eat was
essentially the substitution of the self for God, giving to
themselves (whom they had not created) the law of conduct
in a universe (which they had not created)—a folly to which
today's existential morality is at every moment liable. The
consequence of the ignoring by the man and the woman of
the command was inevitable, and the writer shows it. The
universe, which had been subject to them, blew up in their
faces. They themselves, who had been subject to God, blew
up in their own faces—nothing the world can do to us is as
explosive as what we can do to ourselves, once we act upon
an autonomy for which we have not the qualifications.

> And they heard the sound of the Lord God
> walking in the garden in the cool of the day,
> and the man and his wife hid themselves from
> the presence of the Lord God.

To the perfection of that as a statement of the difference sin makes to our relation with God, nothing need be added.

> The man said, "The woman whom thou gavest to be with me, she gave me fruit of the tree and I ate."
> The woman said, "The serpent beguiled me and I ate."

The man blames the woman, of course. But he blames God too—after all, God had given him the woman, he hadn't asked for one. (The one extra thing sinners now say to God—"*You* made me, so it's your fault"—had not occurred to Adam. It would have been interesting to hear the answer.) The woman blames the serpent. The serpent blames no one: God did not interrogate *him*—if indeed he was Satan, then that particular interview between himself and God had already happened. We note that in our first introduction to the serpent we are told that God had made him, had made him good therefore: what had made him an enemy of God? The rest of the story is of the punishment of the three involved. To the serpent, God said:

> "Cursed are you above all cattle,
> and above all wild animals:
> upon your belly you shall go,
> and dust you shall eat
> all the days of your life."

The sentence pronounced continues faithful to the metaphor —the tempter had tempted as a serpent and is sentenced as a serpent. One remembers the numbers of unbelievers who have laughingly asked how the snake was supposed to have moved before being thus reduced as a punishment to going

on his belly. And indeed there have been learned men, far
removed from laughter, informing us that there are indeed
pagan sculptures in which a serpent is shown standing up-
right "and none in which a serpent is shown on its belly." I
think we need not trouble about either the mockers or the
learned. The metaphor explains the word. The tempter has
already broken with the God who had made him: by this
new sin he falls lower still. The sentence carries the metaphor on:

> "I will put enmity between you and the woman,
>   and between your seed and her seed;
> he is to crush your head,
>   while you lie in wait for his heel."

I will put. Thus the enmity between the serpent and the
woman is not in the nature of things as the human dislike
of snakes is. It is placed there by God. What does this mean?
It may simply be that Eve's friendship with the Tempter
needs God's aid to overcome it. More likely perhaps that
temptation's attraction for mankind needs a continuing
counter-action: perhaps the phrase means that conscience is
strengthened as a kind of instinctive judgment against the
evil course.

The Hebrew version and the Septuagint Greek both use
one verb for what is done to the serpent's head and the man's
heel. The trouble is that it is hard to think of one verb that
will express damage to both head and heel without abandoning the metaphor. One English translation uses "bruise" for
each, but how does a snake bruise a man's heel? It seems that
there are two similar Hebrew verbs, one of which means "to
crush," the other "to lie in wait." We cannot be certain that
the original writer meant to use both: all we can say is that

it would have gone admirably with his metaphor if he did.
Believers naturally tend to see in all this a first promise of
Redemption for mankind. No such promise is verbally there,
only a threat of danger to each. Is there any point in the
damage being to the serpent's head, whereas it is only to
mankind's heel? Hardly: that represents what normally happens when man and snake meet, the snake goes for the foot
(especially bare or sandal-shod), the man for the head.

We note that Paul seems to hold to "crush" for the serpent:
"The God of peace crush Satan under your feet speedily"
(Rom. 16.20).

What is clear is that the writer saw that the conflict between evil and humanity, or rather between a personal force
of evil and humanity, would continue; and he felt certain
that, God being God, he would not have created a world in
which evil would have the final victory, utter the final word.
But he knew enough of past and present to know what a
fluctuating conflict it would be. And he could not see how
the issue would come about.

The Vulgate says that it is the women that will do the
crushing—a slip on the part either of Jerome or the copyist,
a slip in which devotion to Mary of Nazareth took much
delight. But, even with this corrected, one is puzzled by so
strange a phrase as "the seed of the woman." It is not totally
without parallel. Eve herself says of the birth of Seth that
God has given her another seed (Gen. 4.26). And we have
"the seed of Rebekah" (Gen. 24.60), but this was said by
friends of Rebekah before her marriage to a man they did
not know—it is unofficial, so to speak.

We should have expected to hear mankind called the seed
of the man. His non-mention here leaves us with a question.

God had cursed the serpent. He does not curse either the
man or the woman, only the ground in which the man is to
labor. In Scripture God never curses either a man or a

woman. For Eve there was a double result—she would be
mother and wife as God had planned, but with a difference,
diminishing the joy of each.

> "I will greatly multiply your pain in
>   childbearing;
> in pain you shall bring forth
>   children,
> yet your desire shall be for your
>   husband,
> and he shall rule over you."

Every phrase of this is worth close examination. What it can
mean, every woman will document from her own experience
—which can be anything from a balance of happiness to
something wholly agonizing. What seems clear is that the
dominance of her husband is not in the nature of things, it
is a result of the Fall.

The sentence upon Adam similarly meant the continuance
of his first function, but this also in the labor, the travail,
which in all subsequent experience goes with it. In the beginning he had been placed in the garden, not for dalliance
or cultured idling—but to "till it and keep it." He should
continue to till the earth out of which he was taken, but an
earth "cursed" because of him, no longer co-operative: the
agricultural life is admirably summarized—thorns and thistles
and sweat (it could have been written by the Greek Hesiod,
who in his own way regarded the farmer's life as a curse).

One further element in the sentence concerned them both:
they would return to the ground—"You are dust, and to dust
you shall return." When the writer has God say to Adam,
"In the day that you eat of it you will surely die," he knew
that Adam did not simply sin and drop dead: he meant that
with this sin they would lose the immunity from death that

God had meant for them, death would have dominion over
them, and it is with the sentence of death that he ends God's
statement of how mankind, having chosen autonomy, is
henceforth to live it. The new order begins with banishment
from what had been their world.

> Then the Lord God said "Behold, the man has
> become like one of us, knowing good and evil;
> and now, lest he put forth his hand and take
> also of the tree of life, and eat, and live for
> ever"—therefore the Lord God sent him forth
> from the garden of Eden, to till the ground from
> which he was taken.

The words in quotation marks are puzzling. "Like one of
us," for instance. "Us"? We seem to be back at the phrase
we met in the first chapter—"Let us make man in our image
and likeness." Does it mean God and the angels? And if so,
how could the shame and fear in which the pair stood after
their sin constitute likeness to God or angels? One can perhaps see in the next words, about the tree of Life, the truth
that in the state to which they had reduced themselves the
tree of Life was not for them. But nothing is clear.

The reader will read the passage according to his reading
of the whole episode, which includes the picture he has
formed of the writer. My own inclination is to agree with
those who feel there are fewer difficulties left if we see it as
plain irony, rather like the irony of God's answer to Job. Job
had wondered how his sufferings could fit with the justice of
God—as Léon Bloy could say to God, "I would not treat a
mangy dog as you treat me." God retorts to Job, "Were you
there when I laid the foundations of the earth: who determined its measurements—surely you know!" (38.4). He is
mocking Job, who from the abyss of his ignorance, is ques-
tioning the decisions God makes in his omniscience. Here

in Genesis God seems to be mocking the pitiful ambition
which had been the motive of their sin. The Serpent had
promised that they would be like God: now God makes his
comment—"Like God? Look at them." Is God, then, de-
riding the vanquished? Surely the derision is the writer's,
his anguish as he measures the gulf between man's ambition
and man's achievement.

> He drove out the man; and at the east of the
> garden of Eden he placed the cherubim, and a
> flaming sword which turned every way to guard
> the way to the tree of life.

Life as we know it has begun—for Adam and Eve. Eve's
new subjection is underlined—we are told only of Adam's
expulsion, that she went with him is simply assumed—what
else could she do? The paradisal state is over. And not only
for these two. The Yahwist has been trying to account for
the human condition as a whole—given that God is what he
is, why are things as they are? He closes this part of his story
with the cherubim and the sword of flame turning every way,
holding Paradise closed to all. What mankind's state was as
the result of the first sin he tells in the next eight chapters.

The story is sheer tragedy. But the conclusion is not
despair.

Between the condemnation and the expulsion, the writer
inserts two statements so surprising at this point that we
wonder if they have been misplaced. But in different ways
each shows hope not dead. Life still stretches before them—
"the man called his wife's name Eve, because she was mother
of all the *living*"; there is something stunning in Adam's
choosing this moment to name her with that name of honor.
And God had not abandoned them—that is surely the meaning of his making "for Adam and his wife garments of skins."

Does the writer think of Adam and Eve as those particular individuals? For the moment I am not asking whether all mankind is in fact descended from one pair, but only what Genesis is saying. The garden is metaphor. Are the gardener and the gardener's wife? We observe that the word "Adam" means "man" and in all this story of Creation and Fall it is not used as a name—always "the Adam," the man, as his wife is always "the woman." "Adam" is not in the story as a name but only as a common noun; the word Eve is not there at all till just before the banishment. The man is spoken of as Adam only after they have left Paradise, when "he knew his wife again and she bore a son and called his name Seth" (Gen. 4.25). This indeed is the last thing we hear of his doing: he begets Seth, and we see him no more. If Paul had not written as he did to the Romans and the Corinthians, I wonder if the question of the descent of all from the first pair would have arisen? And what does Paul hold?

For the moment I note that there is an astonishing universality about the story. Even a critic who convinces himself that the human race has no one common ancestor would not be inclined to flip the story aside. The man and the woman are Everyman and Everywoman—I had almost said Everyhusband and Everywife. But their everyness is wider than that. The non-scriptural Second Book of Baruch says it for us—Every man is his own Adam.

And whatever the detail of its happening, man and God *are* at two, not at one.

NOTES

1. From Pritchard, *The Ancient Near East: An Anthology of Texts and Pictures.*

6

Sin Takes Over

In chapters 4 to 11 the Yahwist presents the world resultant from Adam's sin. He does it in a series of scenes—Cain's murder of Abel, Noah and the Flood, Noah and his sons, the Tower of Babel—apparently only loosely connected, but in fact as organically related as the four acts of a play. Of the four actors in the earlier play, only two are involved in this one, namely Man and God. The Serpent does not appear, nor the Woman—no significant part is played by even one woman. One remembers Joseph Conrad's phrase (in *Heart of Darkness*, I think) that in the authentic struggles of men, women have no part. If we continue to think of these chapters as a four-act play, the leading character is Sin. Man and God alike move to the rhythm of Sin, man to its commission, God to its punishment and counteracting. Sin provides the continuity.

Abandoning a simile which grows difficult to manage, we note that the writer set out to describe the disorder which was the New Order. He did not know the details, any more than in his account of the Fall. He used stories traditional, legendary, as he found them to his purpose. "Oriental

111

folklore," Hilaire Belloc called it; and some of it was: in this solitary instance Belloc seemed not to see that folklore can preserve truths which history's solemn self-assurance has been known to overlook.

Our writer did not know the details, but he knew the world—his world, ours. The sin at mankind's origin was the hole in the dyke; all the rest. came through, and at flood speed. "The man who commits sin violates order: sin of its nature is disorder" (1 John 3.4, K). At the beginning God had brought order out of chaos. And now there was a worse chaos, in the hearts of men. To Cain (Gen. 4.7) God had spoken of sin as a demon "crouching at the door. Its desire is for you, but you must master it." Cain did not master it. Who does?

The first sin had been from the twisting of the self out of the right relation to God, the desire to act God to oneself: its name is pride; disobedience was the fruit but pride was the root. The second sin was envy, the self twisted out of the right relation to other men. God had approved of Abel's sacrifice and disregarded Cain's, so Cain killed Abel. Was it merely chance, or a very profound insight, which linked the envy and the resultant murder with the altar? Religious wars are notably ferocious, yet the ferocity is seldom because of God, there is invariably more of outraged self in it.

So the picture grows—out of envy fratricide, carried off with arrogance: "Am I my brother's keeper?" Out of arrogance the blood feud, Lamech's seventy-seven fold killing to avenge wrong done him. Civilization grows, sin grows faster —"the imagination of man's heart only evil continually," sin swollen so enormous that God repents having made man. We think of all four episodes as traditional, and perhaps they are, but only of the Flood have we any knowledge that there actually was a tradition; if the Yahwist was using an earlier

Cain and Abel story, we do not know what it was. There are
in all literatures stories faintly, but only faintly, like that of
Noah and his sons. The only Babylonian element in the
Tower of Babel is the tower itself, not why men built it or
what happened to it, or the diversity of languages that
ended it.

The context of the Cain and Abel story is an inhabited
world, with a division already existent between the agricultural life and the pastoral. There is the hostility between the
farmer and the herdsman which threads history; one remembers the high improbability of the song in the musical *Okla-
homa*, "The farmer and the cowboy should be friends." For
the Jews, sheep and cattle men, the farmer had to be the
villain, so God approves the herdsman's sacrifice not the
farmer's, and the farmer kills the herdsman. God punishes
him; he is to give up tilling the earth he has stained with
blood and become a wanderer on its face—the land of Nod
is named from a word which means "wandering." But with
the second sin as with the first, though God punishes he does
not abandon. He will protect Cain from those who would
murder him.

The first murderer, indeed, seems to have prospered. He
went on to found a city (cities also being foes of the pastoral
life). To his descendants we owe the introduction of the
shepherd's life (a little hard on Abel, we may think), of the
musician's, of the blacksmith's. We are given the names of the
next five generations of his sons, down to Lamech, the first
man to have two wives: they are Adah and Zillah, the first
women after Eve whose names we are given. To them he
sings the great boast—he has slain the man who had wounded
him, he will slay up to seventy-seven fold. Interesting that
he should have been the father of that righteous person Noah,

who is the key figure of all this period for the Yahwist, and indeed for the Priest.

For in Chapter 5 the Priest returns—to provide a more respectable ancestor than Cain for Noah and Abraham and the whole Jewish people. Adam had lost both his sons—one murdered, the other banished. So—he "knew" his wife and produced Seth (the name means "replaced"). The author picks up the Hymn of Creation with a one-sentence summary, gives us a line from Seth, through Lamech, to Noah and his three sons.

And with Noah we come to the Second Act, the Flood. But before this we have an odd insertion—how "the Sons of God saw that the daughters of men were fair; and they took to wife such of them as they chose . . . and they bore children to them" (6.1-4).

There is plenty of discussion whether this means that angels had intercourse with women and (though Genesis does not say so) produced Nephilim (the word means "mighty ones"). No one seems clear in his own mind as to what these four verses are saying. I wonder if the writer knew. It is quite possible that he found them, in one tradition or another telling of the sons of El, symbolized by the Bull (pastoralists, therefore), intermarrying with daughters of the earth goddess; and having found them he simply put them in here as a special example of the universal sinfulness which moved God to send the flood.

That there had been a vastly memorable flood is certain, so many peoples retain memories of it. The compiler found two versions—one J, one P, the critics think. Earlier than both was the account in *Gilgamesh* (based on the Sumerian story of Ziusudra). Clearly they are related in detail, yet with enough differences to suggest that all of them were drawing on a version earlier still. The compiler does not try to dove-

tail the J and P stories: there are differences between them
(as between each and *Gilgamesh*) in the measurements of the
ark, in the number of animals taken aboard, in the length
of days the Flood occupied, in the birds sent out. Evidently
the differences did not bother him (any more than he would
have troubled if he could have foreknown that the largest
set of dimensions would have made the Ark about the size
of St. Peter's, and that even that would have been too small
to take in, comfortably, the 600,000 species of living creatures). He did not think details of this sort, or any sort, had
any bearing on the story he was telling. Nor have they. Certainly the elements in the story which alone make it worth
his telling or our reading are not from any existing tradition. They are unique.

In *Gilgamesh* there is no moral motive for the decision to
destroy the whole human race—simply Enlil, the storm god,
felt like doing it. In other mythologies there is the same total
arbitrariness. (The Canaanites had the story of a goddess who
decided to destroy all mankind: to stop her, the gods filled
a bucket with beer and stained it red; she drank it greedily,
thinking it was blood: so she fell into a highly intoxicated
slumber and mankind was saved. But this reads not like part
of a myth but as the production of a writer having fun with
a myth.)

Nor in *Gilgamesh* is there any moral reason why Utnapishtim and his family are chosen for survival—the god Ea
happened to like him: Enlil was furious when he learned
that these people had not perished. But Noah was chosen
because he "was a righteous man, blameless in his generation." This has no parallel in the myths nor could it have;
sinfulness in the Judaeo-Christian sense is not a primary
concern of the gods, only sins against their own dignity,
arrogance or neglect of the rituals. What Genesis gives us is

an utterly unique insight into what we may call the psychology of a God concerned with man; he has God thinking
aloud:

> The Lord saw that the wickedness of man was
> great on the earth, and that every imagination of
> the thoughts of his heart was only evil
> continually. And the Lord was sorry that he had
> made man on the earth, and it grieved him to
> his heart.

For the first time we have God's heart and man's heart
mentioned together. Following God's notably detailed in-
structions, Noah and his family and specimens of every living
thing, of all flesh (J and P give different numbers), enter the
Ark (the word is the same as for the—presumably smaller—
basket in which the infant Moses was launched on the Nile).
With the Flood over and the Ark grounded, we come upon
a reminder of *Gilgamesh*: Noah offers sacrifice, as Utnapishtim had done; God "smells the pleasing odor"—as the gods
had done. But there is quite a difference. We remember that
"the gods, cowering like dogs, crouched against the outer
wall of heaven" when the flood was at its worst. That ghastly
female Inanna "wailed like a woman in labor." When they
smelled the roasting flesh of the sacrifice "they swarmed about
like flies"—as well they might, there were some four thousand of them. Whoever has seen flies swarming over meat
will not feel that the gods were at their godliest.
    Yahweh's reaction to the "pleasing odor" was not of that
happily gluttonous sort. He made a kind of New Year's reso-
lution. He said to himself:

> "I will never again curse the ground because of
> man, for the imagination of his heart is evil from

> his youth: neither will I ever again destroy every
> living creature as I have done."

In other words God, in judging us, allows for our weakness. It is the principle that underlies Christ's "Judge not, lest you be judged." Only God can be trusted to judge us, for only he knows each one's weakness. God goes on to a repetition of the Hymn of Creation. He blessed Noah and his sons, and said to them: "Be fruitful and multiply and fill the earth." But there are certain differences—animals, birds, fish are to be in fear and dread of man (had the writer in mind the animals which fled from Enkidu after his sin?); vegetarianism was no longer demanded of fallen man—he may eat animals. But "flesh with its life—that is, its blood —you shall not eat." Then came the "covenant" with Noah and his sons. "Never again shall there be a flood to destroy the earth": and the rainbow is to be a token of the covenant.

So we are shown the race as beginning all over again. What we may think of as the Third Act begins:

> The sons of Noah who went forth from the ark
> were Shem, Ham and Japheth. Ham was the
> father of Canaan. These three were the sons of
> Noah; and from them the whole earth was
> peopled (9.18f.).

And now we have the second vegetable to be actually named in Genesis (the fig was the first). Noah planted a vineyard. Did his father, Lamech, mean this when "he called his name Noah, saying, 'Out of the ground which the Lord has cursed, this one shall bring us relief from our work and from the toil of our hands' " (5.29)? It reads like a pleasant tribute to wine. Even if Lamech did not know that his son was to plant the first vineyard, the Yahwist clearly had it in mind!

It is a mild curiosity that the first sin named in the New Beginning is drunkenness, making its first appearance (not, I imagine, that we are to believe that before the Flood all men were teetotalers, any more than all were vegetarians). I do not think that the Yahwist saw the patriarch's drunkenness as sinful. "Noah was the first to plant a vineyard"; when he had the first experience of drinking wine he would not have known that it was loaded!

The rest of the story is curious; one gets the feeling that something has been left out. Noah, drunk, lies naked. His son Ham sees him and tells Shem and Japheth: it is they who cover him with a robe, averting their eyes from their father's nakedness. When Noah is sober enough to be told the story, he cries out, "Cursed be Canaan—a slave of slaves shall he be to his brothers." He is to be Shem's slave, he is to be Japheth's slave. Why Canaan? It was Ham, his father, who had been guilty of irreverence: and indeed the combination of the belief that it was Ham who had been doomed to slavery, and that Negroes were descendants of Ham (neither of which things does Genesis say), has been told by devout men from that day to this. But Noah laid the curse on Canaan, not on Ham. And why so ferocious a curse? Slavery for all the offender's descendants outdoes his father's seventy-seven fold vengeance; and that at least was for killing, this for irreverence. It looks as if Genesis does not give us the whole story. There are those who think (without any evidence save intuition) that in the original story Canaan had castrated Noah, as the gods had so often castrated their fathers—there was a Hittite myth that Anu's son had so treated Anu, by biting, had laughed and been cursed. If I were forced to make a guess, it would be that the curse *was* directed against Ham, and that Canaan was substituted either to justify Israel's enslavement of the Canaanites or to express Israel's abomination of Canaanite abominations.

The Noah episode ends with mankind beginning anew from Noah's sons, nations sprung from them spreading through the world speaking their own languages. It is the first appearance of nations, and Genesis clearly sees the nation state as a new source of evil, of pride especially—men facing God, outfacing him.

That, I take it, is the point of the Tower of Babel story, which is the Fourth Act of the Yahwist's drama. In the light of what we have just been reading, its opening is strange: "The whole earth used the same language and the same speech" (11.1). The Yahwist was quite capable of seeing the verbal contradiction, but this opening was necessary for the point the story is to make. Nothing could indicate more clearly that he was telling it as a parable. If "Once upon a time" is not written all over it, there is at least a touch of the feeling of a moral tale. And the point it makes justifies its place in the drama.

In the writer's mind, obviously, were the fascinating Ziggurats of Babylon: he may even have been thinking of the temple Gilgamesh built—"They raised the head of Esagila towards Apsu" (here, the sky). But Babylon has nothing even vaguely like the Genesis story.

The builders are not shown as setting out to challenge God:

> "Come, let us build ourselves a city and a tower
> with its top in the heavens, and let us make
> a name for ourselves."

It is the ignoring of God that our author sees as so frightening—the mightiest building in their world built not for God's glory but their own, much as the mightiest buildings in our world are not for God's glory but man's financial profit.

E

God sees a threat in it that the builders were not conscious
of—the threat of the absolute state, growing to world stature:

> "This is only the beginning of what they will
> do; and nothing that they propose to do will
> now be impossible for them. Come, let us go
> down, and there confuse their language, that
> they may not understand one another's speech."
> So the Lord scattered them abroad from there
> over the face of all the earth.

The story is the Yahwist's commentary on the meaning of
Babylon, and until the last book of the Bible, Babylon is *the*
enemy of God. Whether we take the ending of the Noah
story or the Tower of Babel story we have a world totally
disunited—men separated from God and from one another.
We are ready for Abraham, and to Abraham we are introduced (11.26), with God promising that "in you all the nations of the earth will be blessed."

Am I reading more into chapters 2-11 of Genesis than is
there? Everyone must read for himself; we cannot know what
was in the mind of this long-dead man of genius, but what I
have written here seems to me the minimum meaning of
what he wrote. He did not know the details of man's beginning on this earth, and so had to write figuratively. But
unless the things he is telling us in figure had a reality of
their own, then nothing is accounted for, we are left without
clue as to the gap between what mankind in fact is and anything that God could conceivably have wanted men to be.

7

The Doctrine of Original Sin

WE MAY OR MAY NOT believe in a sin at the beginning of human history affecting all men till the end of time. But here, anyway, we are—in a world surely not as God wants it, members of a race which is a mess: with the mess getting, if not worse, at least more complicatedly bad; and no great consolation to be got from looking at ourselves, each one of us a microcosm but each one a microchaos too. The problem that occupied the Genesis writer is still with us. Whatever God had in mind in creating the universe, it could hardly have been this.

Humanity quite evidently needs healing, remedial work on an inconceivable scale, practically re-making: it might seem almost better to wipe out the human race and start over again; indeed it looks as if the race might wipe itself out, leaving the field clear for nature to try something different. One remembers George Bernard Shaw's suggestion that the working class should be abolished and replaced by sensible people; there are moods in which one wonders why so constructive a suggestion should stop with the working class. Nor is this a freak of a satirist's fancy. The writer of Genesis 6 may not have fully entered into God's mind, but he expresses his own to us when he tells of God "grieved to his heart that he had made man on the earth," and saying, "I will blot out man . . ."

But God was not King Lear, stunned at man's ingratitude and raging at it. He had made men out of love: they needed healing, and out of the same love he would provide it. Through Christ, God has told us what the healing is. The words for it are Salvation, Redemption; the mode of it is Re-birth. The master text for the doctrine of original sin and Redemption, without which it cannot be understood at all, is John 3.3—"Unless a man is born again, he cannot see the Kingdom of God." We are born into a race in need of healing, we are to be re-born into Christ. We are to be lifted from being the kind of men we are by birth into being the kind of man he is. Or rather, into a beginning of that: for Redemption—like our own humanity and the race's—is given to be grown into. "Just as we have borne the image of the man of dust, we shall also bear the image of the man of heaven." This *is* Redemption—"I am in my Father, and you in me and I in you" (John 14.20). Re-born into Christ, indwelt by Father and Holy Spirit as he is, we are a new being—with the new life and the new powers of action that go with the new being. We have in us the powers, if we will use them, to move towards the right use of self and away from the wrong use; and this in relation not only to God but to man and to the whole of Creation. Only with that clearly grasped can we understand what the sin at humanity's origin meant, and how the condition from which we needed to be redeemed grows out of it. Only in the light of what Christ did for its healing can we cope with the problem of how man's disorder began and grew rooted.

I

How much of the Genesis story goes back to Moses we cannot tell with any certainty. But there is no mention of Adam in any Scripture written before Genesis 2; and no mention of him after it till the Jews returned from their captivity in Babylon (round 540). With the begetting of Seth he vanishes from our gaze. His name is at the head of the genealogical table with which 1 Chronicles opens, much as we find it at the head of the genealogy of Christ as Luke (Paul's companion) gives it. There is a possible mention in the book of Job. Otherwise the Hebrew Bible knows him no more. Sirach refers to him: "All men are built of the same clay, son of Adam is son of earth" (33.10, K). Wisdom has the same idea —all have "come down from that first man that was a thing of clay" (7.1, K); and there is the statement that Wisdom watched over "the lonely father of this created world" (10.1, K).

Eve fares no better. One gets the impression that she would not have played any decisive part at all in the Genesis story but for the writer's awareness of the place of sex both in sin and in life. In the wonderful Ezekiel vision of Paradise restored, Eden is clearly being used as an archetype, but there is no mention of a woman in it. Eve is mentioned by name only in the book of Tobias—"You made Adam from the slime of the earth and gave him Eve as a helper and support" (8.8, D).

It all amounts to very little. Adam and his Fall had not taken hold of the Old Testament mind. The writers show no more interest than the Egyptians in the origin of man, and they have not the Egyptian interest in the origin of the universe. The founding of the human race with Adam was too remote; it was not of present and continuing concern like the building-together of the Jewish people with Moses. And it is not in the Gospels.

The absence of any reference by Christ to the connection between his own redeeming action and mankind's fall in Adam may surprise us. He does not mention Adam at all. His one clear reference to the Genesis story has to do with the original establishment of marriage as monogamous— two in one flesh, joined by God, not to be sundered. He seems to refer obliquely to the Fall when he calls Satan "a murderer from the beginning . . . a liar, and the father of lies" (John 8.44), for Satan had lied to Adam, and Adam, believing the lie, had brought himself and the human race under the doom of death. But even here he is not talking about Adam, only about Satan; and in any event he does not link this up with his own sacrifice on Calvary.

Christ's whole concern, in fact, is with what we are redeemed *into*. He goes into no detail as to how the disorder originated, which we are redeemed *from*. His emphasis is all upon how men are to be saved and the new state in which the saved are to be. He assumes that they know they need saving: it must be obvious even to themselves that they are lost. The question comes spontaneously from one of them: "What must we do to inherit eternal life?" (to be echoed, verbally at least, by the "What shall I do to be saved?" of Paul's jailer at Philippi). Christ lavishes all his utterance upon the answer—like a doctor who does not tell his patient how he got the disease but how he is to be rid of it. Something stands between men and their soul's health; he shows them himself as at once physician and healing and health. Born into their own life, they must be born again into *his*, so that they may nourish their lives with his. He is united to God; united to him, they will be united to God too.

But for Paul we should be hard put to it to find in the New Testament, any more than in the Old, the connection between mankind's redemption and the sin of Adam. Yet, though no other New Testament writer mentions it, Paul, writing not only to the Church in Corinth where he had lived and labored, but also to the Church in Rome which he had not yet visited, takes it so very much as a matter of course that it can hardly be some new insight special to himself. He is assuming not simply that the new Christians have read the first chapters of Genesis; he sets out certain truths, flowing from the Genesis story but not obviously contained in it, and he treats these not as if they required demonstration, rather as if they were contained in the teaching these two Churches had already received.

What would the Genesis writer have made of Paul? And indeed of the New Testament generally?

"The Lord God made the earth and the heavens" (Gen. 2.4). As we have noted, the man who wrote that could not have said "The Word was with God and the Word was God, by him all things were made," as John did; he could not have spoken of "a Son *through whom* also he created the world" or of "the Image of God *through whom* and *for whom* all things were created" (Col. 1.16; 1 Cor. 8.6). In Romans and Corinthians we shall find the Genesis story as the first writer knew it, but with developments unknown to him. Consider a handful of verses from Paul:

Romans 5.17: *If, because of one man's sin, death reigned through that one man,* much more will those who receive the abundance of grace and the free gift of righteousness reign in life through the one man Jesus Christ.

18: *As one man's trespass led to condemnation for all men,* so one man's act of righteousness leads to acquittal and life for all men.

1 Corinthians 15.21: *As by a man came death,* by a man
has come also the resurrection of the dead.

22: *As in Adam all die,* so also in Christ shall all be made
alive.

45: *The first man Adam became a living being;* the last
Adam became a life-giving spirit.

47: *The first man was from the earth, a man of dust;* the
second man is from heaven.

48. *As was the man of dust, so are those who are made of
the dust;* and as the man of heaven, so are those who are of
heaven.

49: Just as *we have borne the image of the man of dust,*
we shall also bear the image of the man of heaven.

We might almost speak of the first Paul and the second.
The first would have accepted without surprise the opening
part of each of these verses—even, I think, the whole race as
involved in the sin at the race's beginning; he does not say
this in so many words, but it is the state of mankind as a
whole he is seeking to account for, and he does speak of Eve
as the mother of all living, does show Paradise closed to men.
What the second Paul says of death incurred through sin is
verbally no more than the first said: and the first would have
seen that if death was to be vanquished, it could only be by
restoration of life. Did he see sin as death in the soul, even
though bodily life continues? Would he have seen—not as
fully as the second Paul, but seen *at all*—the two lives and
the two deaths? Would he have seen what Christ was to mean
with his "Do not fear those who will kill the body but cannot
kill the soul; rather fear him who can destroy both soul and
body in hell" (Matt. 10.28)? The doctrine of Sanctifying
Grace, supernatural life, is hard to find in the Old Testament: a feel for it is there, just as for the Trinity, but in its
fullness supernatural life can be seen only as union with God

in Christ, and this involves too much that had not been revealed to the men of the Old Testament.

And there we come to what would have startled the first Paul—delighted him, no doubt, as he came to grasp it, but surely startled him at first hearing—I mean the second part of each of those verses. He had seen a conflict, in which the seed of the woman would ultimately be victorious: but he had not seen what the victory would be. What indeed did the antagonists mean to him, the Serpent, the Seed of the Woman?

Clearly he saw the Serpent as a personal force of evil, not equal to God and doomed to suffer God's punishment. But what did he, or any Jew of his time, really know of fallen angels, of the Devil, of Satan? But at least the first Paul would have felt that Christ's words on the Devil—"a murderer from the beginning . . . a liar and the father of lies" fitted the story he himself had told of man's fall. And though the book of Revelation was not talking of the fall of man when it spoke (12.9) of "that ancient Serpent who is called the Devil and Satan, the deceiver of the whole world," he would have found the phrase apt to his own serpent.

Indeed the New Testament takes the Serpent with all seriousness. What John says of the reason of Our Lord's coming—"The Son of God appeared in order to destroy the works of the Devil" (1 John 3.8)—fits with what Paul told Herod Agrippa as the reason that same Christ sent him to the Gentiles—"that they may turn from darkness to light and from the power of Satan to God" (Acts 26.18). It fits too with "The God of peace will soon crush Satan under your feet" (Rom. 16.20) and with "He himself partook of the same nature, that through death he might destroy him who has the power of death, that is the devil" (Heb. 2.14).

Paul, the only one of Scripture's writers known to have

been bitten by a snake (Acts 28.3), does not explicitly use the word serpent in what he says of Adam's sin. But it is hard to feel that he had not clear in his mind the Genesis phrase about the seed of the woman crushing the serpent's head, when he wrote of humanity's pre-redemption childhood— "we were slaves to the elemental spirits of the universe. But when the time had fully come God sent forth his Son, born of a woman, born under the law, to redeem those who were under the law so that they might receive adoption as sons" (Gal. 4.4).

We may conclude this glance at the first Paul and the second with a return to the first Adam and the Second—born of God, born of a woman, *the* seed of the woman whom the first Paul could not have foreseen. We may doubt if any phrase of the second Paul would have gripped the attention of the first more than "Adam who was a type of the one who was to come." It grips our attention certainly. In the Old Testament we find suggestions of One to come, prefigured by historical persons like Moses, David and Elias, as well as by more mysterious personalities like Daniel's Son of Man, and the Suffering Servant of Isaiah—but not by Adam. Clearly it was not as first sinner that Adam was a type of Christ, but as first man of the first creation. Christ was to be the be-ginning of a new creation, a new beginning, a new order (2 Cor. 3.6; 1 Cor. 5.7; 2 Cor. 5.17; Gal. 6.15).

Adam's fall is told in Genesis with a kind of splendor, but the given details are of a simplicity which is either merely naive or richly mysterious. Paul saw it as the sin of the race, creating a breach between the race and God; God and man had been at one, they were no longer at one; at-one-ment was necessary. We can hardly say that these truths lie clear on the story's surface. Nevertheless, taught by Paul, we can read Genesis as telling of a catastrophe at humanity's origin, shadowing and conditioning its whole history, bringing the God-man to his death on Calvary. There are people who find all this improbable. But then, as we have said, man is improbable. Compared with the highest animal he is incredible.

II

"Original Sin," like so many of theology's technical terms, can mislead. It misled Freud, who thought libido largely synonymous with concupiscence or original sin: but original sin is not concupiscence, it is the reason why that admirable quality is out of control. Indeed it can mislead even theologians when they are off their guard. One of them, for instance, calls it the collective processing of individual man by the accumulated sins of history and culture. But original sin is not this "processing": it is the condition under which we are exposed to it.

In its commission, original sin was a choice at humanity's origin of self as against God, making a division between God and the race of man. We, who had no part in its commission, enter life as members of the race thus sundered. We begin in the condition in which the first sinner began again after the Fall—having natural life but not sanctifying grace, God holding us in existence, as he holds the lower animals and the rest of creation, but not indwelling us any more than he indwells them. "Original sin"—the effect in us of the sin at humanity's origin—is this absence of God's indwelling, the lack of righteousness which, as the Council of Trent phrases it (Session VI ch. 3), "follows natural birth precisely as righteousness follows regeneration."

Pause upon "indwelling." In all beings whatsoever God is

present by his power holding them in existence. But to spiritual beings God offers a profounder presence, a personal union of himself with the person each one of us is. We call it indwelling and it is not fanciful to see it as God making himself at home in us. Christ Our Lord uses those precise words: "If a man love me, he will keep my word, and my Father will love him, and we will come to him and make our home with him" (John 14.29).

Thus indwelt, man is a new creature (2 Cor. 5.17). A body-enspirited is a different reality even as a body, a man-indwelt is a different reality even as a man. The life proper to such a man is the new life into which we must be re-born: it flows into action as faith and hope and charity. We speak of it as supernatural life; but in truth it is the natural life of the indwelt man. About God's first presence, by which we and all creatures are drawn out of nothingness, we are not consulted, we have no choice. We have no way of refusing it either as to its beginning or its continuance. A man may refuse God's love finally and everlastingly, but God is still there, holding him in existence. But indwelling is by invitation—offered by a sponsor if we receive it in infancy, maintained by us unless we decide to opt for self: in which event indwelling ceases. It is a fearful thing to have nothing of God but his presence, refusing all the other gifts which men as creatures need and which only he can give.

As we have seen, the foundation text is neither in Genesis nor in Paul, but in John. We must be born again. The doctrine can have little or no meaning for those who either do not know Christ's teaching on the second birth and the second life into which it ushers us, or who do not attach the importance to it that Christ himself attached. There are those who feel that the doctrine can be both modified and developed in the light of scientific knowledge not available when it was formulated; and there are others who feel in their bones that it wholly lacks present relevance. Either way there is gain in knowing what the doctrine actually is.

Paul harmonizes with and develops Genesis. The Church harmonizes with and develops both. We have noted that the Genesis writer might have been startled at the light Christ shed for Paul on Adam's sin. Paul, I think, would not have been startled at the Catholic doctrine of the Fall. Let us look at it.

God created man for man's sake. If we think of God as the Absolute, as Pure Act, infinite in beatitude as in all perfections, creation was an act of infinite altruism. He could create only for man's sake, not his own; in that sense he has no sake! But this is philosophy at its barest. Scripture's God is not of that infinite remoteness. God is love, and love is not like that. Love not only loves, but wants a return of love. This is one thing God wants of men, one thing men can give God or refuse him. There is no care in God. That is a truth of philosophy. It does not mean that he does not care. He created out of love: he saw men as capable of existence, capable of rejoicing in existence, and he gave them existence. In his beginning, man was united to God by a union of his will with God's because love is in the will.

God created man for man's sake: that is one truth. He created man for himself: that is another. It does not contradict the first, but enlarges and perfects it. Creating man for himself was not a piece of infinite egoism; it was the supreme thing he did for man. He had made animals, men, angels; he made animals for men; he did not make men for angels—not to serve angels, not to find completion in knowing angels and loving angels. The intellect of man will attain its plenitude in knowing God and being known by him; the will in loving God and being loved by him; the whole man in living union with God. To have been made for anything but God would be a diminution. Nothing less than the infinite is good enough for us: God made us for himself.

As the Church sees it, the first man, and the first woman equally, were created with the natural life of soul and body—body enspirited, or spirit embodied, as we may choose to see it. But there was one difference between the natural life as they received it and as we receive it. For death was not in God's plan. Of itself, the human body, like the animal to which it is so evidently akin, will ultimately wear out, even if it is not broken by violence or eaten into by disease. One way or another the body will, in the course of nature, reach a point at which it is no longer capable of responding to the life-giving energies pouring into it from the soul. Death to us seems natural. But Paul and the Church teach that for our ancestors God saw to it that nature should not thus take its course. God would see to it that the body retained its full power of response. But on a condition—"in the day that you eat of the fruit you shall die." If man sinned, nature would take its course: not that he would fall dead, but that he would become subject to death.

Sin seems to us as natural as death. Here too God provided the one condition which might make the avoidance of sin a possibility—not a certainty, for man's will is free, but a possibility. He gave the first man the gift we call integrity, that is wholeness, the elements in man rightly related to one another in a being rightly related to God. These gifts, integrity and immortality, we call preternatural, a special extension of powers naturally present.

Reading Genesis, I feel as Paul did that immortality and integrity are there and would have remained but for sin. That is the Church's feeling too. At the end of the fourth century, the Council of Carthage, for instance, says we must not say that Adam would have died even if he had not sinned.

Certain other of the gifts called preternatural—knowledge, wisdom and freedom from suffering—listed by theologians have not been officially taught by the Church. The first two were on Trent's agenda, so to speak, but the Council never got round to them. Where Paul and the Church go deeper than Genesis is in the meaning they give to the death ushered in by sin, a meaning which could not be clearly visible until after Christ had revealed the newness of life he had come specifically to bring: "I am come that they may have life and may have it more abundantly" (John 10.10, D). He is not promising length of days and freedom from disease in the life into which all men are born: he is speaking of a second birth, a second life therefore: "unless a man be born again of water and the Holy Spirit, he cannot enter into the kingdom of God" (John 3.3, 5, D). This is the life which Paul relates to Adam's sin—"If, because of one man's sin, death reigned through that one man, much more will those who receive the abundance of grace and the free gift of righteousness reign in life through the one man Jesus Christ" (Rom. 5.17).

So the Church sees it. The life by which men are men was not the whole story for Adam and his wife, and is not meant to be the whole story for any of us—had it been, what death would Christ have overcome? There was the second life penetrating the first. Paul calls it "grace," "free gift," or simply "life," the Church "sanctifying grace," "supernatural life." (As Luther's doctrine of grace differs from ours, his doctrine of original sin differs too—this complicates our discussions with Protestant theologians.) In it we can move towards our ultimate goal, reach it, possess it. God enters man to abide in him, says Christ: to make his dwelling in him: man is a new creature, no longer man simply, but man-indwelt. Here upon earth his new life means a new level of union with

God as truth, God as love. At death it means a fullness of union in which at last man is fully man, every element of his humanity in action upon its highest object. This second life is not simply a passport to heaven, allowing men in. The life of heaven cannot be lived without it; because the direct vision of God which is the essence of life there calls for powers that natural man has not got, only man-indwelt.

As the Church sees it, man at his beginning was wholly united with God. God did not create man with natural life and then add supernatural life. Man as God brought him into existence was man-indwelt—faith and hope and charity as natural in him thus indwelt as intelligence and will in man as man. Integrity was a natural consequence of union unviolated—body subject to soul, the lower powers of the soul to the higher, natural habits to supernatural, the whole united with God-indwelling.

In man's will the union stood, in man's will the union was broken. Satan promised the first pair that if they disobeyed God's command, they should be as God themselves. Thus prompted, they set their will upon autonomy. The decision was catastrophic for themselves and for all men till the end of time.

Consider themselves. They lost the supernatural life, fruit of the union with God which their sin had snapped short. Love of God, issuing in love of neighbor, is the vivifying principle of sanctifying grace: love of self had annihilated it. From their souls had gone the life without which the vision of God at death was not possible. Supernaturally they were dead. They were left with natural life only, but even this not as it had been. Man's natural liability to death could have its way: integrity, harmonious interworking of man's powers, could be only a mocking memory.

Man's powers and desires had maintained harmony because all alike were directed towards God as their supreme end: now they no longer had one end to unify them, hold them in harmony. Each must pursue its own devices, one seeking its satisfaction in one direction, one in another. So that the soul was faced at once with the rebellion of the body and warfare within its own powers.

The first sinners had wanted autonomy—to want it is a recurrent folly of mankind; Byron's line "Lord of himself—that heritage of woe" is no bad summary of human history. Finitude unsupported, which is man's state with God bowed out, is poor equipment for autonomy. By the first sin, the sinner's humanity was not simply damaged by misuse: it was abandoned, damaged, to its own inadequacy.

How much adequacy is possible to finitude unsupported? We are the only creatures who have to make those two near-contraries, spirit and matter, function as one being—each of them a potential principle of chaos. The Devil might well have rubbed his hands when he realized the opportunity God had given him in making man.

There is the limitation in our intellect—so much that we do not know, so much that we know wrong: no agreement among us even about things essential to intelligent living together—about God and about man and about the world in which we find ourselves, with which we must cope, which we must one day leave. For what destination?

There is imagination, the picture-making power, meant to be a useful servant to the intellect: in so many of our judgments imagination practically takes charge.

There is the high probability of chaos in the will. We can be torn any number of ways at once by desires mutually exclusive. The passions harry man perpetually. That man should have passions is natural, he would be a poor thing without them: what is tragic is that they should dominate.

Before the Fall, we remember, the first pair were naked and not ashamed. Sexual passion was not their master. Their first recorded action after the Fall was sexual intercourse. "Adam knew Eve, his wife, she conceived and bore Cain"— the first murderer was the first fruit of sexual passion uncontrolled. At this point, as at every point, the Genesis writer knew what he meant to tell us.

And sex misused is not the most destructive of man's powers. It was said of the old League of Nations that it was a league of kettles on the boil. So, potentially and often enough in fact, is every human grouping—family, state, casual groupings of every shape and size.

The first sin meant catastrophe not only for those who sinned; it involved the whole race. The union between those first sinners and God was broken, the union between the human race and God was in that fact broken. Mankind was no longer at one with God, heaven was closed to it. The race had been at one with God as a son with his father: now it stood facing God as a servant his lord. And so it remained until the eternal Son of God remade the sonship.

III

There are those who feel that the doctrine of atonement involves the psychological monstrosity that we all deserve punishment because Adam did wrong, and reward because Christ did right. Thus one theologian writes that it is entirely offensive to suggest that one man's moral status should be determined by the action of another with whom he has never even indirectly come into contact.

There is a misunderstanding here. The Church does not teach that Adam's guilt becomes personally ours: what she teaches is that his sin altered the conditions in which each of us must receive our life and live it. Nor does she teach that we are saved simply because Christ died and rose again, but only that in so doing he created a new situation in which each man, Christ aiding, is to work out his own salvation ("with fear and trembling," says Paul, who had so evidently feared and trembled). In Karl Rahner's fascinating phrase, Adam's act at the beginning of human history took root as a "fatal a priori."

That one man's action can change the conditions of life for others, can create new situations affecting others profoundly, hardly needs saying. The whole human race is living differently because of Albert Einstein, to say nothing of Adolf Hitler; the whole Christian world is living differently because of Martin Luther. But whereas we can see why Einstein's discovery and Hitler's war and Luther's revolt changed things for all of us, we cannot so clearly see why Adam's disobedience and Christ's obedience did so. For Einstein and Hitler affected men's relations with one another and with the material universe: the chain of causes and effects is under our gaze. Luther affected men's relations with God and so with one another: the chain of causes and effects is largely under our gaze. But Adam's sin and Christ's sacrifice involve God's purpose in creating the human race, and God's mind is not under our gaze: Paul is not the only one with reason to know that his ways are unsearchable. Why God reacted as he did either to the sin or to the sacrifice we have no explicit statement from God, and no experience of being God, to tell us. But what followed because he saw the one and the other as he did, we do indeed know.

Whether men were to have God's indwelling and the life consequent on it as a matter of course, so to speak, receiving grace along with their manhood—this question God allowed to be decided for the whole race by a success or failure at its beginning. Why he chose it so he has not told us, but through

Paul he has told us that it is so. In the beginning humanity
was a graced humanity, wholly at one with God. By sin the
union of love on which grace depends was broken. There
was a new situation: men would be born into a race divided
from God, born with human life only, grace still to be received and not certain to be received.

Men had lost nothing to which they had any claim. They
were still men—in a general way they were the kind of men
they would probably have been if God had not made that
first venture of a wholly graced humanity, but had started
each man off as man and nothing more, with grace somehow
to be won by each.

But God would not leave them so. He still wanted mankind to be at one with him. Expiation must be made for
the sin which had broken the oneness—not because God
wanted vengeance, but that the order which sin had broken
might be restored by that sin's reversal.

So Christ came—God's son, wholly equal to him, wholly
God. He became man, made our nature his, and in it made
human nature's expiatory offering. He made not only expiation but atonement—our pronunciation of the word hides
its meaning, which is at-*one*-ment. He created a new situation. By birth we are at one with Adam and enter into the
situation produced by his disobedience; by re-birth we are
made at-one with Christ and enter into all the rich possibilities of the situation produced by his obedience. But in
either situation our virtue or guilt lies in the choice we ourselves make.

Why God chose to act and re-act as he did we can only
speculate. But there is one clear implication which we must
not miss. God saw the race not only as a convenient name
for millions upon millions of human beings, but in some
sense as an entity in its own right. Between it and himself a

breach had been made: while the breach remained, the most
virtuous man was still a member of a severed race, a race to
which heaven was closed. The first sinners may very well
have repented, and received supernatural life into their souls
once more: it would not be in its first richness because of
the damage done to the individual nature of each—body
and soul at war, the soul's powers in conflict among themselves. But with whatever richness of grace, they could not
have entered heaven at death, because their race was no
longer at one with God. Man, in other words, is not a self-
contained unit: each man has his own private and personal
relation with God, but it is in this larger context of member-
ship of the race.

John the Baptist called Christ "the lamb of God" who
would take away *"the sin of the world."* No one had ever
used that phrase before. Yet upon ourselves it hardly reg-
isters—we have it in our Mass as the *sins* of the world. For
each of us there is the gruesome list of his own sins. But
even with the Baptist's phrase to help we are hardly aware
of a sin of the race.

We need to concentrate on this idea, so out of our way
of thinking is it. We can get some small light on it by thinking of a solidarity with which we *are* familiar. A poisoned
finger may cause the death of the whole body—distressing,
but no one finds it surprising. A foot slips and the whole
body plunges to destruction. The mind makes decisions
registered in the brain, and every part of the body is affected
for good or ill. The solidarity of the body sufficiently explains
all these things. There is a similar solidarity in the human
race, not so tight-knit or clearly visible, but real.

As I have said, it is out of our way of thinking. We have
no natural, spontaneous reaction to the idea of the human
race itself—not only all men living, but all who have ever

lived or ever will live. It goes with our limitation that we
find the whole race of man too large, too dispersed through
space and the millennia, to be loved or even realized. Because
of this limitation we find something almost grotesque in the
idea that our whole race was involved in what its first members did or failed to do. But, it would be strange if God, who
is equally the creator of all men, in whose image all men are
made, to whom no man is more immediately present than
any other, did not see the race as a whole and treat it so.
That he does so is the primary fact about the human race.

The problem for the race was the restoration of oneness.
And only God could restore it. It is one of the more tragic
facts about man that he can destroy what he cannot rebuild
—can kill, for instance, and not restore life to his victim.
Man could break the supernatural oneness between man and
God; he could no more re-make it than he could in the first
instance have made it. Only God could do either.

We may feel it hard that the solidarity of the race should
involve ourselves, innocent bystanders, in the catastrophe—
indeed not even bystanders, only innocent. Second thoughts
are clearer. Which of us would care to take a stand upon his
innocence? Our record in face of such temptations as have
come our way gives us small ground for assurance that we
should have done any better than our first father; we have
all on our own account set our will against God's, we have
all played at being God, making for ourselves the law of our
action. All the sins of all men since Adam have followed
the pattern of Adam's sin, and make a sort of solidarity in
sin between him and us which is a horrid parody of the
solidarity in nature. The race has endorsed Adam's sin. He
is one parent we all resemble.

In any event the solidarity of the race is a fact like the law
of gravity; a given man may complain of gravity when he is
falling from a height, but all men would find life on earth

impossible without it: just so, the solidarity of the race brings us far more profit than disadvantage. It would be agreeable to have only the advantage of our oneness with all men, strengthened by their strength, not weakened by their weakness, but laws are not like that. Solidarity must either exist or not, once existent it operates. And on the balance we are quite immeasurably the gainers—in detail and in sum. By solidarity we fell with Adam; by solidarity we can rise with Christ.

8

Science and Genesis

THERE HAS BEEN a way of "doing" Redemption as if Adam's Fall, the Sin at the origin of the race, is practically the whole of it, with Christ's Death and Resurrection coming in simply as a kind of happy ending. But this is to get the proportion totally wrong. We need to be redeemed from our present condition, *no matter how we got this way*. If we had never been told of first parents, the redemptive action of Christ would still be there. He can save men who have never heard of Adam, or who dismiss him as a legend.

To ignore this primacy of Christ and concentrate everything on Adam was, I have said, to get the proportion wrong; and there is no compensating advantage because the elements on which the main emphasis thus came to be laid were a complication in their own right, and seemed to lend unreality to the Redemption itself.

I call them a complication; they are a tangle of complications. In the first place people were left wondering what connection there could be between a sin so long ago and ourselves who so evidently had no part in it (one heard the objection summarized as "Eve ate the apple, we get the

143

stomach ache"). From the beginning this was a difficulty. And in the last hundred years came Evolution raising a dozen others—notably two: the solid rejection, by the scientists mainly concerned, of the idea of a first couple; and the improbability of the first men to cross the animal border being in a paradisal condition.

People who up till then had believed found themselves with a stricken feeling that the doctrine of Redemption is built on the sin of Adam, and Adam has been blown sky-high. But it is built on the Death and Resurrection of Christ, not on the sin of Adam. Christ has not been blown sky-high. Has Adam?

I

Was Adam one individual man, the ancestor of all men? Those scientists who work on human origins, most of them at least, find it difficult to see the human race as all descended from one couple. Men trained in palaeontology, anthropology, genetics, are practically unanimous in feeling that the frontier between animal and man could not have been crossed by one single individual or pair from whom all the existent races of men have descended. They do not assert that this can be proved; but with minds immersed in all the relevancies, in possession of all the knowledge at present available, they find monogenism unacceptable—everything, they say, points the other way.

For those not trained in any of these fields such a unanimity must carry great weight. But can we simply accept it? We lend them our ears, we cannot give them our minds—if for no other reason than that they cannot give us theirs. They cannot give us their experience, the years of training and testing which have strengthened and enriched their minds,

the habits grown instinctive, the reactions grown spontaneous. We can but weigh as much as they can convey to us of
reality as they see it. We can no more simply swallow scientists than we can swallow historians or philosophers or
theologians.

What we are hearing is the scientific orthodoxy of today,
but scientific orthodoxies, like religious, have been known to
change. The Physics I was taught as a boy—from Newton
to Clerk-Maxwell—was serenely confident and wholly convincing. I remember a teacher who taunted us—wouldn't we
little Christians like to have as conclusive a proof of God's
existence? And we had to admit that we would indeed! But
today's schoolboy can correct Newton and Clerk-Maxwell
in the light of Einstein's correction of Newton's laws. No
one holds this as a blot on Newton's name—without Newton,
no Einstein. But it reminds us that scientific orthodoxies,
like religions, can change. About the cradle of every science,
said Thomas Huxley, lie extinguished theologians like "the
strangled snakes beside that of Hercules." Surely extinguished
scientists are as frequent. In his *Process of Organic Evolution* Professor Stebbins tells us that anything written on
Evolution before 1950 is obsolete (which suggests a vast number of extinctions).

And it is not as though we have settled into a long era of
Einsteinian peace to match the three centuries of the New-
tonian. There is the linear view, probably held by the majority, that our universe is expanding and will ultimately
move towards a state of maximum entropy, an inertness
equivalent to death. But there are those who hold that this
is true only of its present expanding phase and that there
may come a contracting phase—why not? After all, we do
not know what started the expanding phase! In this view we
are very close to the pagan idea of eternal recurrence.

Upon polygenism, anyhow, scientists *are* unanimous, or

nearly. Yet the question still stands—how binding upon the non-specialist is their unanimity? When they say that "everything" points to a particular conclusion, what do they include in everything? Their work, like that of all specialists, has developed certain of their mental powers, but has left others considerably less used; they have a microscopic knowledge of their chosen area, and a sureness in it; they and their fellow-workers speak the same language, have grown into similar ways of seeing and thinking, and this is a great strength: it would be a real wrench to introduce a non-scientific factor. To allow the descent of all men from one pair would go against all these mental habits. But belief in God, in immortality, in God-made-man are not among those habits; we cannot be certain of the judgments, even the unanimous judgments, of minds which omit so much.

I have just spoken of their minds as immersed in all the relevancies; can we, can they, be sure that God and Immortality and Incarnation are not relevant? In these they are not *as scientists* immersed. A geneticist tells us that the emergence of a single pair is "infinitely improbable"; if we have followed his arguments we may agree, but with a proviso "unless God intervenes." Is God's intervention improbable"? Our geneticist may very well be irritated, even if he happens to be a Christian: God is not part of his scientific habit. To his scientific formation, so much has been contributed by the insights of men who would regard God as irrelevant. And it goes with the scientific habit to feel safest with views which can be tested experimentally—as God's intervention at Man's origin hardly can—or mathematically.

The reason why scientists rule out descent of all men from one pair is *not* that the differences observable in the races of mankind demand a variety of original human ancestors. Quite the contrary. It seems to be generally agreed that men, whatever their race, are all variants of one same species, *homo sapiens*; and the inclination is to believe that they all come from one single animal stock. Then why such a complete rejection of one single human pair? Not principally because of a conviction that a single pair would not have survived long enough to get the human race safely established and on its way. The principal reason is that, especially since Mendel's work on genetics, it is held that Evolution operates not in individuals but in populations, groups of interbreeding individuals.

In a book such as I am writing, genetics presents an insoluble problem. To write clearly about genes would take space far out of proportion to their importance as I see my theme. To write briefly is to be incomprehensible. So far no one seems to have been able to write of them without diagrams which I find harder to comprehend than words. I shall simply say as much as my theme demands, hoping that it will later be seen that it demands no more. (Anyone really interested will find the whole subject superbly discussed by G. Ledyard Stebbins in *The Process of Organic Evolution.*)

According to what we may call standard evolutionary theory, new species result from an accumulation of small mutations over vast intervals. Genes carry the heritable characteristics. In a given organism, some of the genes may be altered, apparently by chance (a scientific friend thinks the changes happen because a cosmic ray strikes a molecule in the nucleus—this also being by chance). Usually the mutation damages or destroys the embryo in which it manifests itself. Very rarely it is advantageous. It continues to be transmitted. After many generations, maybe covering thousands of years, the creature having it undergoes a favorable mutation of a different sort. So that its descendants now have two advantages over their more normal contemporaries. The accumulation—chancy, as we see—piles up. At last one is born with a sufficient number of the mutations needed for a new species. At first he interbreeds with the population to which he belongs: but his descendants gradually draw apart, a new species exists breeding true and no longer capable of interbreeding with the cousins it has grown away from. One theory is that the individuals which possess the necessary mutations outlive and outbreed the others—the doctrine of the survival of the fittest is now in operation. Mutations, one gathers, are unpredictable, but the ratio of their occurrence is, statistically, fairly standardized. And they can be produced in the laboratory by radiation, for instance: but there is considerable disagreement as to the conclusions to be drawn from mutations thus produced.

In its general outline Evolution is part of the common knowledge of twentieth-century man. The earth's crust, he learns, solidified 3500 million years ago. Life appeared perhaps a thousand million years after that, definitely in the next thousand million as shown by fossils—of plants, for instance. All life so far was in the sea, and it remained there for the next couple of hundred million years, roughly half of the Palaeozoic (ancient life) Period which scientists call Primary. Three hundred million years ago there is evidence of the first amphibians—fish, with four fins which could be used vaguely as legs, staggering about on land: from those four fins came the legs of all the quadrupeds, and our own legs and arms.

Not so many million years after that came the reptiles, creatures up to fifty tons, whose world it remained for the 150 million years of the Secondary Period. With the Tertiary, beginning 75 million years ago, the great reptiles are extinct and the mammals in command: round the middle of the

Tertiary came the apes, with whom our interest in Evolution naturally quickens. Ape fossils go back 40 million years: in the next 20 million they are spread widely in Africa: and if the scientists are right, from one of these ape-stocks came man.

The pictures we are given of the passage from ape to man are pleasing—I give one, but there are others equally "pleasing." Anthropoid apes took to the trees, releasing the forelimbs from walking so that the legs began to be arms, the feet to be hands; as hands made it unnecessary to use the jaws for hanging on, the jaw muscles diminished, allowing the brain to grow; as the brain grew, the skull became round, bringing the eyes forward and closer . . . and so on . . . and so on. Yet so slight is the bodily difference between men, who have crossed the animal frontier, and the apes, who have come right up to it, that biologists classify them as of one family.

There, in a three-paragraph conspectus, are the chapter headings of the story of Evolution. No one pretends that there are not vast gaps in the evidence: a scientist, cross-examined by a skilled lawyer, might not convince a jury. Transitional types have been found between genera and species, for instance, but not between phyla; simply at a certain period there is one phylum, and long after there is another which might very well have evolved from the former, and the assumption that it has evolved from it casts light upon much else. It may be that this power of casting light is the strongest evidence of Evolution's truth. In the phrase of Teilhard de Chardin, it gives "a vision so homogeneous and coherent that it is irresistible." I know no one who resists it, not I certainly.

But all who *accept* Evolution are not thereby *affirming* it. Indeed, for the non-scientist to affirm Evolution would be

faintly ridiculous. It is not enough to have read summaries
of the multitudinous evidence which has convinced scientists.
One must have practised the sciences. The scientist is in what
has become his natural mental habitat. He is at home in it,
we are casual visitors. The thousands of millions of years of
our earth, for instance, the thousands of millions of light
years of our universe, have a reality for him; to us they are
simply rows of noughts.

I have read dozens of popularizations with a sort of stricken
admiration. Here and there are facts whose significance even
the amateur scientist can see—as that "all bodies owe their
origin to arrangements of a single corpuscular type," that by
so many patterns and formulas man's structure is akin to
those not only of the whole animal and plant world but of
the inorganic as well. But at the end of all my reading, the
only conviction genuinely my own is that the whole thing
could not possibly have been by chance, a mind and will must
have been in action, a conviction the pure scientist may find
irritating! I would, if I were a pure scientist.

By Revelation we know that it was not by chance. The
universe is not simply an accident which happened to happen
and men simply parts of it. There was a mind which meant
it and had a purpose in it. When the theologian "accepts"
Evolution, how does he relate it to God as creator and con-
server? If he is a wise theologian he knows that he cannot
watch God in action. He can know what God has told of
himself, he can see the universe.

God acts in eternity, in one single timeless operation of
wisdom and love, not watching men and things to see what
note is being played wrong, that he may instantly play the
notes that will harmonize the world's discord into concord.
God acts where *he* is; all elements of creation receive the
effects where *they* are. He acts in the spacelessness of his
immensity and the timelessness of his eternity; they receive

the effects in space and time. There is something splendid in the way scholastic theology has built scholastic philosophy into itself. But it can have a hypnotic effect, so that the student thinks he sees it all, when he can at most have flashes and glimpses. We have not experienced eternity, we cannot know what infinite knowledge actually is. Without revelation we should never have guessed that the infinite simplicity of God was Triune; there may be similar fruitful surprises about eternity.

The theologian asks himself how all that the scientist tells him fits with as much as he can comprehend of revelation—asks himself not as expecting to see the whole answer, happy if he can see the question better.

Without the will of God nothing receives existence or continues in existence. God has a purpose in bringing it into existence. The theologian can conceive God as making provision for the realization of his purpose not by "intervention" at key points, but by what he has made each thing to be, by the laws he has set for the being and growing of the universe as a whole, and for the being and growing of each element in it. This development goes on. But of the details of his provision for it God has not told us; we can only think about them, praying for aid in our thinking. We take two great "moments"—the appearance of life (after how many thousand million years?), the appearance of man (after how many more?). Did God so establish the original elements that life and man should simply emerge when things sustained by him had developed into readiness for them? Or was there something like a new "creation," the divine action lifting things beyond anything which could flow solely from their development?

In their answers theologians differentiate between "life" and "man." Up to modern times, most of them probably thought that living beings could issue from non-living with-

out any special intervention from God. St. Thomas thought
so: clearly there is nothing contrary to orthodoxy in thinking
so. It is simply a question of fact. If life ever is produced
in a test tube, St. Thomas will smile. The theologian of
scientific mind, rejecting what to him seems only discontinu-
ity, opts for the first answer in relation to humanity also:
he accepts God, but his whole tendency is to exclude intervention by God—interferences with the great rhythm of
reality. He may be right. But one such "intervention" the
Catholic cannot write off—I mean the Incarnation.

II

Thirty million years ago there were manlike apes; thirty-five
thousand years ago there were men unmistakable. At what
point between are we to place man's actual arrival? Not-men
and not-quite-men, in the millions of their years, are not
theology's immediate concern. It is with *man* that the drama
of Redemption begins. When did *he* arrive?

Scientists studying fossils vary in the evidence they regard
as decisive of the human threshold crossed. There are what
the fossils themselves show—walking erect, for instance, or
brain volume, or whether the bone structure would have
allowed speech. The shaping of tools clearly marks a decisive
advance—between the first hominoids to be discovered and
the first shaped flints lie a quarter million years. Do any of
these things mean that man has at last arrived?

One's answer depends upon what one thinks man *is*. *Homo
sapiens,* the scientist calls him. "Rational animal" the philosopher of the scholastic tradition calls him. The "sapient"
of the one, the "rational" of the other, cover the same observed phenomena—the phenomena we find attributed to
man in Scripture, which gives no definition. From the be-

ginning Scripture's man knows and wills, can be talked to and discussed with, questions himself and God: he is held responsible for his decisions, indeed he holds himself responsible—he can repent, make restitution. This, at a minimum, is the man that Scripture and Theology are about: and these attributes are the "rationality" of the philosopher, the "sapience" of the scientist.

At the root of it all is that man not only knows, as an animal does: he knows himself as a man, is conscious of himself as himself, knows that he is knowing. He can form mental concepts, by which things are present to his mind as what they are: and his concepts are not only of the particular individual but generalizable without end: they can even be abstractions. To me, all this is evidence of a spiritual element in man by which he is made in God's image; but even one who makes no such distinction of matter and spirit at least sees it as lying *above* the line between men and animals.

To return to our question—when was the line crossed? It is hard to feel certain, with the scantiness of present evidence. As one scientist puts it—"The crying need of the moment is less guesswork and more fossils." The four-foot-tall *Australopithecines,* whose fossils are found in Eastern and Southern Africa and may go back half a million to a million years, are usually held to have been apes: they were bipeds, could walk erect, though it seems to have been hopping rather than walking: their cranial capacity varies from sub-gorilla to just above; there is some evidence of tools: if they had speech it was scarcely articulate. Remains have been found recently in Tanganyika which may or may not have been of Australopithecines, may or may not go back close on two million years. *Pithecanthropus,* named by joining the Greek words for ape and man, is hard to place either in date (from a quarter million to half a million years ago) or in the evolutionary line: he had tools, fire, and a cranial capacity higher

than the Tasmanian aboriginal who was still there till we
wiped him out a century ago. In my boyhood *Pithecanthropus
erectus,* recently discovered in Java, was getting vast pub-
licity as the missing link. (When they were trying to teach
me Geology at Sydney University, all the excitement was
about the Piltdown skull, which turned out to be a fake.)
With *Neanderthal* man—ape forehead, tools, fire, burial
flowers—the question seems to be not whether he was man,
but whether he was in the main line of development or a
sideline which came to an end twenty-five thousand years ago:
some scientists hold him not capable of interbreeding with
homo sapiens, others that some of his genes may be in us.

Was man rational, man spiritual, needed for the making
of tools—not simply the use of whatever happens to be handy,
like stones or thigh bones or the branches of trees, but the
shaping of stones or wood in advance of the need to use
them? How near rational action can the animal get? Like so
many borderlines, this one is shadowy. It is hard to be sure
whether tool-making, fire-building, were high points of animal development or the first evidence of genuine rationality,
"sapience." They do not seem to demand the power to form
general concepts: flowers for the dead perhaps do. From concepts and the power to form them flows the whole vast reality
of civilization: the power to form them does not show in
the bones.

But with *Cro-magnon* man, who appeared thirty thousand
years ago, scientists feel no hesitation: he produced a culture
unmistakably human. As we look at the cave paintings—at
Altamira, say, dated fifteen thousand years ago—it would
never occur to us to doubt that the painters were men of our
own sort. Not only that: the art is not new-sprung from a
man of genius; there had to be a long tradition growing
into it.

Whether man arrived thirty thousand years ago, or three

hundred thousand (or, as Louis S. B. Leakey suggests, some
millions), did he arrive solitary or in numbers? There is no
actual evidence, but scientists are, as we have seen, practically unanimous against a first man or a first couple, because evolution is of populations not individuals. (It is
pleasant to remember that in a Sumerian myth the goddess
Mani started off the human race with seven couples.)

Man's evolution, as the scientists trace it, is parallel with
that of all other species, and for these the group is the only
thinkable unit. Scientifically there is no reason to except
man from this invariable process. When a new species is discovered the evidence is found in many parts of the world—
the primates, for instance, from the south tip of Africa to
the eastern edge of China; Pithecanthropus is found in Java
and in China, though with an interval of time between; and
Cro-magnon man covers a fair space of Europe. It is true that
in none of these instances have we the first emergence under
our gaze. Yet to those who are not scientists, the unanimous
view of those who are—that everything points the one way
—is impressive.

But as we have already noted, God might have acted in the
production of man as he had not acted for earlier beings.
Man is sufficiently different from all others to make it not
unthinkable that his origin might not have been precisely
like theirs. Quite apart from what we may call the religious
fact—that God made men in his own image, that he was to
enter into a dialogue with men which should never cease,
that God's only-begotten Son was himself to become man—
there is the difference between what man has made of himself and the world, the dominion he has exercised over it—
a dominion now moving out into space. The emergence of
a first couple may be improbable; but then man *is* improbable. The differences between man's body and ape's body

may be slight. But between man and ape there is a whole
world of difference, a whole universe. I imagine it is a matter
of temperament whether one thinks that a gulf so immeasurable was more likely to have been crossed by one or a number. The evolution of animals may not tell the whole story
of man's.

III

Does Scripture see Adam as one individual man, from whom
all men are descended, whose sin affects all? This reduces
itself to the question whether Paul sees him so. If he had
only the story in Genesis and casual comments made on it
here and there in the rest of Scripture, Adam and Eve might
very well have stood for Man collective and Woman collective. But it is hard to think that Paul did not regard Adam
as a single individual, as was Christ of whom Paul saw Adam
as the "type"—"As one man's trespass led to condemnation
for all men, so one man's act of righteousness leads to acquittal and life for all men" (Rom. 5.18).

That sounds decisive. Yet it may not be so. Nor may the
reason Paul gives for calling on woman to be silent in church
—namely, that Eve led Adam astray (1 Tim. 2.14). At all
times it has been common to refer to well-known fictional
characters as if they were real. We do it ourselves—any good
detective would be flattered to be compared with Sherlock
Holmes; many a man out of touch with present reality has
been called a Rip van Winkle; beyond counting are the in-
decisive rulers who have been called Hamlets. When
Khrushchev spoke of the kiss of Judas, he was not expressing
belief in the Gospels.

We can find instances in the New Testament. Christ said:
"Jonah was three days and three nights in the belly of the

whale, so will the Son of man be three days and three nights in the heart of the earth" (Matt. 12.40). This is not taken by Catholic scholars as settling the question whether Jonas is history or parable: the comparison would have served Our Lord equally well either way. Similarly in Adam, Paul had found, and seemingly was the first to find, a perfect antitype for Christ. Did he believe that Adam was a single individual? My guess is that he did: though my further guess is that, even if he had not, he could still have balanced Adam and Christ in the same way.

If Paul did believe Adam was one man, would his belief be decisive for us? It is a delicate question. When James talked of the patience of Job (1.11), was he binding us to believe that the book of Job was reporting actual conversations about afflictions actually suffered? When St. John wrote, "Cain was of the evil one and murdered his brother, because his own deeds were evil and his brother's righteous," he may very well have taken the story of Cain and Abel quite literally. But most commentators see it as a story concerning a much later time—a time when there actually were pastoralists and agriculturists—which the Genesis writer linked with Adam as telling of the first sin after his, his being pride, the first sin in relation to God; the second being envy, the root of evil in relation to our fellow men.

What would Paul have thought? He would hardly have thought of himself as deciding a question which had never occurred to him, or indeed to anyone else. What of Scriptural Inspiration? That depends on whether Adam's sin is of the essence of what Paul was telling, or only an illustration-by-contrast. I certainly do not think it is for me to settle. What has the Church made of it?

There are two key documents—the decree of the Council of Trent (1546), and the Encyclical *Humani Generis* (1950).

Trent first. No more than Genesis or Paul does Trent ac-

tually say that all men have Adam for ancestor. What it says
is that original sin "has its source in a sin actually committed
by Adam and conveyed—*transfusum*—by generation so that
it is present in every individual." This certainly means that
we are affected by Adam's sin by being born into the human
race. Does this imply that all are descended from Adam?

One's immediate answer, I think, is Yes. On second
thoughts one might modify this slightly to the conviction that
the Fathers of Trent would not have phrased it like that if
they had not believed in Adam as ancestor of all. But does
this make it part of the Council's authoritative definition?
That is for the theologians to discuss: Karl Rahner thinks it
does not. In *Theological Investigations* he argues that while
the Bishops almost certainly believed it—having no more
knowledge than Paul of the reasons geology and the rest
would one day bring forward to question it—what they defined was that original sin is involved in the solidarity of
the human race, of which we are members by generation.
They were condemning a thousand-year-old Pelagian error.
Why should they have bothered about it? Perhaps because
it had recently been repeated by Erasmus. The error naturally was not Polygenism, the theory that there were many
first ancestors, not one single pair: that possibility had no
more occurred to Pelagius or Erasmus than to the Bishops.
The error was the denial of a sinfulness, or liability to sin,
given us with our nature, and the consequent assertion that
we sin in imitation of Adam, not because our natures are as
they are because of him. Had the Bishops had to treat of
Polygenism, they might well have condemned it too. But they
did not, and their authority lies not in what they would have
taught, only in what they taught.

Humani Generis, having said that we are free to hold our
own views as to the evolution of man's body, goes on to treat
of Polygenism. It is against. The relevant paragraph begins

with the statement that upon Polygenism the Church's children do not enjoy—*"minime fruuntur"*—the same liberty as upon Evolution; it goes on to say that believers in Christ cannot hold "either that after Adam truly human beings existed on the earth who did not come by natural generation from the same first parent of all, or that the word Adam signifies some kind or number of original ancestors." So that Polygenism is condemned. Yet not, I think, with an absoluteness that closes every door forever. For the reason given is that "it is not clear that such teachings can be reconciled" with the revealed and Church-taught reality of original sin. Indeed between the first version of the Encyclical and the form in which it was issued there was the hint of a tiny crack —"it is clear that it cannot be reconciled" was changed to "it is not clear that it can." What if such clarity could be attained?

Meanwhile the Church holds on to Adam and Eve as real persons in whose single catastrophe we are all involved. But she does not otherwise linger on them. Thus, it is the general view that they repented of their sin and regained God's friendship. But the Church does not say so. If we want to know the place that events occupy in the Church's mind, the attention she gives them in the Liturgy is a safe guide. And she does not build Creation and Fall into her liturgical life as she builds Incarnation and Redemption: there is no Feast (with octave) of the Creation of Adam or the Emergence of Eve (the Decostation of Adam, one supposes).

Quite apart from what the Church teaches, my own personal inclination (it is no more than that) is for descent from one pair—the gap between the highest animal and man is so enormous, if we consider the whole man and not the body only, that the idea of creatures streaming over it seems incredible: it is hard enough to conceive of even one. Thus I do not prefer descent from one pair because the doctrine of

Original Sin would collapse without it, as I once thought. Like most Catholics, I had fallen into a way of thinking which ran something like this: we are all descended from the first man, and what he lost he could not transmit to us—we could almost hear our Apologetics teachers say Q E D.

This being assumed as inescapable, ingenious efforts were made to establish the physical descent by generation of all from one. Eve presented the first problem, since Adam did not generate his own rib. The theory that Adam and Eve were conceived in the womb of a not-quite-human mother did not show her as descended from him. The theory that Adam had sexual intercourse with a not-quite-human female and she conceived Eve at least meets that difficulty!

That a sin at the race's beginning should condition the lives of all men till the end of time is mysterious. But it is only to a very superficial view that physical descent from Adam would make it any less mysterious. For original sin means that we enter life without sanctifying grace in our souls, and we do not inherit our souls—each soul is a special creation. Even those Christian thinkers who might not feel sure of this would at least agree that sanctifying grace is not heritable. Therefore, sanctity unviolated in Adam, grace unrejected, is not to be thought of as a *source* from which, but only as a condition under which, grace would have flowed to all men. We should see his obedience as a *condition* on which all who were to be born into his race would have begun life in grace. Because he failed the condition, men would not receive grace—without which they cannot reach the goal meant for them—simply by being men: each could receive it or not according to his own personal response to God's love. To the end of time men will be born members of a race which lost its first oneness with God by a sin at its origin. It does not seem to make a vast difference whether the sin was committed by two or by many. The point was that in its beginning the race chose its own line instead of God's.

How does the possibility of many "first" parents affect the solidarity of the race? The question is academic, of course: that God should see the race as one is what matters, not that we should. But we can let our minds linger on it. We remember that for the Jews a "son" need not have been generated by his father—formal adoption gave a man not only a new father but all the new father's ancestors. Genealogies in Scripture did not mean necessarily a relation by blood— common interests or even neighborhood would do. Quite apart from that, we might very well think that what all men have in common, namely their being made in the image and likeness of God, is so much more important than the mere flowing of semen from one single body, that we need look no further for the unifying principle of the human race. Be careful of the word "mere" applied to the body: the Manichees would have approved, but not the Jews, especially not the New Testament writers: for though spirit is greater, matter has its own sacredness, the body is not "mere."

Observe how insistent the New Testament is upon Christ's entry into our race by the way of the flesh. We have John's towering phrase "the Word was made flesh," and in two of his epistles John returns to the same fact, especially in the first—"every spirit which confesses that Jesus Christ has come in the flesh is of God" (1 John 4.2). "Flesh," of course, need not mean the body only, but human nature: yet it is always the nature of man *who has a body*. He is "of the seed of David according to the flesh," says Paul (Rom. 1.3, D); he is "the fruit of David's loins," says Peter (Acts 2.30, D). By this we are all his kin. "He who sanctifies and those who are sanctified have all one origin. . . . Since therefore the children share in flesh and blood, he himself likewise partook of the same nature . . . he had to be made like his brethren in every respect" (Heb. 2.11, 14, 17).

Yet, *for solidarity*, a soul-relationship of all men made by God in God's image is of greater importance than blood-relationship. Even we can see it so. It is hard to build our attitude to our fellow man upon common descent from human ancestors of whom the vast majority of the human race has never heard—to say nothing of the animal ancestors all the way back to the pre-Cambrian sandworm whom one has heard mentioned as the earliest ancestor ascertainable.

God, one feels, must see it so. It is what God had immediately in mind in the creation of men—"Let us make man to our image and likeness." Every man bears that likeness, each has his own way of bearing it, no man exhausts the possibilities of likeness; only in the human race as a whole, seen as one reality, does God's purpose grow towards achievement.

IV

The other notable difficulty raised by Evolution is the improbability of the first men to cross the frontier being in a paradisal condition. But what *is* a paradisal condition? To consider this, we must clear away a certain amount of—not litter exactly, fantasy perhaps.

Knowing nothing of what science would one day discover in the realm of protology, Christian writers picture not only a paradise of all bliss but a first man to dwell in it perfect in body and mind, the mind rich with all the knowledge required for a there-and-then lordship of the universe. Between the Old Testament and the New, as we have noted, Jewish writers had let themselves go on the bodily side—Adam seventy feet high, for instance. Christian writers had him at least seventy feet high mentally. None of this is in Scripture —the paradise of Isaiah (61) is in the future; as the story is told in Genesis, Adam and Eve are simply man and woman —in the rest of the Old Testament they are all but ignored. What the doctrine of Original Sin requires is a humanity capable of dialogue with God—men knowing themselves as men, aware of a God whose commands are to be obeyed. There are not many races on earth today so primitive that they could not meet this minimum.

What of God's indwelling, and the infusion of Sanctifying Grace? Missionaries baptize the aboriginal without hesitation. One hears of no race so primitive as to be thought unbaptizable: and all the baptized are indwelt by God unless and until they refuse him. If we feel instinctively that man at his most undeveloped is no strong foundation for a decision which should affect all men till the end of time, at least we are rid of the need of basing the doctrine on original Supermen. Something considerably less splendid, or splendiferous, will do.

But what is the probability of the first men's meeting a requirement even so considerably scaled down? In the total absence of sure knowledge we can let our minds rove about this.

If we accept Evolution, then one thing sure is that there actually was a first human in the sense of one whose parents were not. If a number of them arrived about the same time, each was the first man or woman in his own genealogical line. What did he think of his mother? Or his father, if he knew him?—animals usually don't, and there are primitive men who don't, not realizing that pregnancy issues from copulation. How, and how early, did he realize his difference? What difference did his difference make to himself, to others?

If he had brothers and sisters, were they of his sort or his mother's?

Idle questions these, and there is no end to them. Since there is thinking in our world, there had to be a first thought, a first concept. Was it thought by the first man? Or was there a gradual development (spread over ages?) from instinct, which is all that his parents had, to thinking, which is human? Teilhard de Chardin holds it could have happened only between one individual and the next: he finds it impossible to imagine intermediate stages—"the threshold had to be crossed in one stride."

Then there is language: it is hard to conceive thought without it, hard to conceive more than a rudimentary language without thought. Assuming the first men were born of one of the primates, it would have happened thirty-five thousand years ago: and in that time none of the apes which remained apes has produced a language. Was language the breakthrough which meant that the frontier had been crossed?

Again, though it may seem unbearably old-fashioned to say so, there was a first sin, an original sin in the sense we have been using—the first sinner was doing something no ancestor of his had done, animals don't sin. We tend to lift our modern eyebrows at the gift of integrity which theologians attribute to Adam. But if he had animal ancestors, they really had integrity; animals still have it unless we spoil them of it. They act according to their nature: it is rationality that imposes the strains on integrity we all know so well: only rational beings can misuse reason. Some early human then—the first, one guesses—discovered sin, a discovery as surprising as that of fire (which also displeased the gods). He would have reacted to whatever it was he had done, with pleasure surely, and of course with a sense of guilt—otherwise it would not have been sin.

What ill-action was it that brought the first blush to a human cheek? Was conscience, rather than language, the break-through? How early did it utter its first depressing comment? And when did religion appear, belief in powers beyond man? The belief is pretty universal, no people however primitive is without some form of it: by what process did it establish itself so universally? Was it the inevitable, and therefore universal, reaction of human minds to the universe at a particular stage of development, or—or what?

The first men had to cope with a reality never thus coped with before; how long did their efforts take to develop into the phenomena we know as rationality, language, sin, guilt, religion? Just as the community does not compose music, someone does, so with religion: someone must first have actually bowed before something as sacred—countless someones surely, concentrating ages maybe of feeling and thinking into utterance of the meaning of things. The scientists have done some superb speculating, but they have no actual information to give us. How quickly could primitive man develop the rationality required for oneness with God and its loss, as Genesis tells it, still more as demanded by the doctrine of Original Sin? Skeletons will not tell us. No one finding the bones of an Australian aboriginal, for example, could know the profound religious-metaphysical stage his mind had reached: no one meeting even a living aboriginal would suspect it—material civilization so crude, no seed planted, no animal domesticated, no wheel, no sail, no building.

Upon this matter of the first men we can speculate enjoyably, if with uncertain profit. Thus it seems to me that there is no difficulty in fitting the cave artists of Altamira and the Dordogne valley into the Genesis story, even as developed by the Church. These men can be dated some fifteen thousand years ago. How long before that had the Cro-magnon people developed to this point? We can date their first recognizable remains thirty-five thousand years ago. How close to those

first remains would the Adam and Eve of Genesis be thinkable? The twenty-thousand-year gap is a bare moment in the
whole story of Evolution, but in the development of *homo
sapiens* it is a very considerable time indeed. Our own recorded history goes back, say, six thousand years—how
immeasurably long that feels, what developments and regres-
sions it contains. The time between Altamira and the first
Cro-magnon remains is three times as long; the space is most
of the earth's surface; we have no light on that vast darkness,
no recorded history, precious little of any other evidence. It
would be a reckless man who would assert that any particular
thing could not have happened in that period.

Arguing from this end, there is not much more we can
say. Starting at the other end, we speculate upon the first
human beings and what may have been their level of rationality, spirituality. The problem for the Christian theologian
lies in Paul's placing in one man the sin in which all die, a
difficulty emphasized for the Catholic by the statement of
Humani Generis that all men now in the world are of the
race of Adam. On the face of it this would seem to mean
that the first beings genuinely and fully human were of the
required mental stature. But how did they arrive at it?

There have been attempts of varying degrees of ingenuity
to meet the difficulty. Some suppose tens of thousands of
years during which our ancestors developed so far that when
at last a spiritual soul was infused men were sufficiently advanced for relation with God and a decisive choice of their
own will against his. Some suppose a long infancy of the race,
faintly analogous to the infancy into which all of us are born,
with spirit present but not yet available for use, so to speak.
The Church has not condemned the Scotist theory that Adam
was not given supernatural life at once but only when he
was prepared for it; nor does she seem to have dismissed the
possibility of genuine men who died out before Adam—

leaving only Adam and his descendants to fill the earth and subdue it. Theories that Adam might have come late into the story of man are balanced by others which place him very far back. Origen seems to hold that the Fall took place in a world of spirits before the beginning of the universe, and man's spirit was given a body and placed on earth as a punishment. And there are theologians now who think it probable that the first fossil remains of almost men belong not to Adam's ancestors but to his descendants—at the start of the long climb back to the level from which his fall tumbled mankind. I do not discuss such theories: this book is about Genesis, which does not seem to allow much room for them.

To summarize this chapter: the simple truth is that the modern theory of Evolution is only in its beginnings, and the doctrine of Grace seems to be stirring towards further development. We are not yet ready for a convincing, or even very plausible, synthesis.

EPILOGUE

Beyond Genesis

I

WHEN WE SAY "creation," what are we saying?

We use the word both for the process and the product, for God's creative action and for what exists because of it. My question includes both, but concentrates on the first.

God causes something to be wholly in existence—that is, he makes it not from some already existent thing, as human making must always be, but in its totality. God's will alone brings it into existence, that is creation's prime meaning; but God's will alone holds it in existence, that is creation's inseparable other side. Creation is one complete action in God, but in things created God's action is continuous. If the Creator withdrew his will, the creature would have to rely for existence only on the other "constituent"—what it is made of—nothing. We use two terms, creation and conservation; without conservation, creation would be pointless.

But that is not the only sense in which creation is continuous. We have noted Augustine's view that in the beginning God created the seeds of what was ultimately to be, elements which in the course of the centuries (how many

169

centuries, he had no reason to suspect) would develop into the universe we know. In creating the universe he was not making something but starting something. He made man, for instance—that according to Genesis being the point of the whole venture; and in this too he was not making something but starting something. Before the creature man actually appeared on our planet, if the evolutionists are to be believed, his making by God had been in process for millions of years, millions of things had to happen as they did or the making of man could have been snapped short. Our ancestors had to grow *into* man. When man at last appeared, he had to get to know his environment and cope with it; and in the knowing and the coping he grew *as* man. That is, he grew as the person he individually was, and grew in his relation with others, so that mankind grew. That began how long ago? Thirty thousand years? Three hundred thousand? Millions? For the moment here we are, and we are still only rough sketches of what we are to be, the material out of which beings fully human are to be made. Even had there been no such catastrophe as Christians believe at the race's origin, the growing would still have had to take place; because that is what creation is—a God-directed growing from nothingness at the beginning to completion at the end of time. In this, Scripture broke away decisively from all the religions and philosophies of time circling on itself, with no point of arrival but only endless beginnings all over again.

II

Between man's first creation and his achievement of completion as man, Scripture speaks of two other creations which we shall not find in Genesis.

1. "Neither circumcision counts for anything, nor uncir-
cumcision," says Paul, "but a new creation" (Gal. 6.15). "If
anyone is in Christ, he is a new creation" (2 Cor. 5.17). We
are back at Christ's insistence upon the necessity of a second
birth into a second life (John 3.3).

By nature we are in the likeness of Adam, who was in the
likeness of God. By the new creation, we are "conformed
to the image of his Son"—who is the second Adam, the perfect likeness, whom the first prefigured (Rom. 6.14). What is
the process of the new creation? "As many of you as are baptized into Christ have put on Christ."

There are parallels between the new creation and the first,
both before and after:

(a) It has to be grown *into*. It too had its evolution—
through the pagans, still more through the Jews, in whom
Christ was mysteriously in operation: "Our fathers were all
under the cloud, and all passed through the sea, and all
were *baptized into Moses* in the cloud and in the sea, and
all ate the same supernatural food and all drank the same
supernatural drink. For they drank from the supernatural
Rock which followed them, and the Rock was Christ" (1
Cor. 10.1)—the Rock is told of in Exodus 17.6 and Numbers 20.11.

(b) It has to be grown *in*. While still in the body "we are
to bear the image of the man of heaven" (1 Cor. 15.49). But
that is the beginning of a fuller likeness: "we are being
changed into his likeness from one degree of glory to another" (2 Cor. 3.18).

It is close, tough thinking. I wonder what the new Christians of Corinth made of it as it was read to them. What do
we make of it?

2. "The creation itself will be set free from its bondage to
decay and obtain the glorious liberty of the children of God"

(Rom. 8.21). "According to his promise we wait for new
heavens and a new earth in which righteousness dwells" (2
Peter 3.13.)

"Then I saw a new heaven and a new earth; for the first
heaven and the first earth had passed away. . . . And I saw
the holy city, new Jerusalem, coming down out of heaven
from God. . . . death shall be no more, neither shall there be
crying nor pain any more, for the former things have passed
away" (Rev. 21.1ff).

The Yahwist's problems were sin and death. Christ de-
feated them, but only in the next life will men know life
unending and holiness without flaw. And not only men will
reach fulfillment, but creation too—a new heaven and a new
earth.

The problem here is that men will die, while mankind
continues and the universe continues. For men who die loving God and their neighbor there is the direct vision of
God, and all that issues from that, in intellect and will and
all the soul's spiritual powers. But only with Christ's Second
Coming, and the ending of the first heavens and the first
earth, will fulfillment be total. When will the Second Coming be?

When mankind has reached the fulfillment possible to it
here upon earth: "Be ye perfect as my heavenly Father is
perfect" is Christ's rule for each man: surely it is also his rule
for the race of man. Our ancestors grew *into* man: man
grows *as* man. The Second Coming will not mean the nipping
in the bud of *that* growing, it will come at the full flowering.

We may form our own notion of what full flowering will
be. There is at least a reasonable probability that it may mean
(as Teilhard de Chardin thinks) that humanity has attained
a maximum of unity for the whole species combined with
the maximum development of the personality of each man

in Christ. When will that be? It depends on mankind's use of its powers and conquest of its weaknesses, in co-operation with the Holy Spirit. There will be advances, but retreats and stagnations too. That is why Christ our Lord could say —"of that day and hour no man knows."

Some Further Reading

This is not a bibliography. Upon each topic there are far too many books for a bibliography to be thinkable. The books here listed are for those who wish to carry their study on to the next stage.

On the Old Testament generally:

Peake's Commentary on the Bible. New York, Nelson, 1957.
A Catholic Commentary on Holy Scripture. New York, Nelson, 1953.
The Jerusalem Bible. New York, Doubleday, 1966.
The Jewish Encyclopedia. New York, Reprint House International, 1968.
W. F. Albright, The Bible and the Ancient Near East. New York, Doubleday, 1961.
Ignatius Hunt, O.S.B., Understanding the Bible. New York, Sheed and Ward, 1961.
Alexander Jones, Unless Some Man Show Me. New York, Sheed and Ward, 1951.
Leonard Johnston, Witnesses to God. New York, Sheed and Ward, 1960.

C. H. Dodd, *The Authority of the Bible.* New York, Harper Torchbook, 1958.

G. E. Wright and R. H. Fuller, *The Book of the Acts of God.* New York, Doubleday, 1965.

ON GENESIS:

There are two new and excellent editions: *Genesis: A Commentary* by the Lutheran Gerhard von Rad (Philadelphia, 1961, Westminster Press) and *Genesis* translated with an introduction and notes by the Jewish scholar E. A. Speiser (New York, Doubleday, 1964).

Bruce Vawter, C.M., *A Path through Genesis.* New York, Sheed and Ward, 1956.

Henry Renckens, S.J., *Israel's Concept of the Beginning.* New York, Herder, 1964.

ON THE MYTHS:

Mircea Eliade, *Patterns in Comparative Religion.* New York, Sheed and Ward, 1958.

W. F. Albright, *From the Stone Age to Christianity.* New York, Doubleday Anchor Book, 1957.

S. N. Kramer, *Mythologies of the Ancient World.* New York, Doubleday, 1961.

D. Winston-Thomas, ed., *Documents from Old Testament Times.* New York, Nelson, 1965.

Christopher Dawson, *The Age of the Gods.* New York, Macmillan.

Christopher Dawson, *Religion and Culture.* New York, Sheed and Ward (Meridian, paper).

Robert Graves and Raphael Patai, *Hebrew Myths.* New York, Doubleday.

R. T. Rundle Clark, *Myth and Symbol in Ancient Egypt*. New York, Grove Press, 1960.

S. G. F. Brandon, *Creation Legends of the Ancient Near East*. Mystic, Conn.; Lawrence Verry Press, 1963.

Philip Freund, *Myths of Creation*. New York, Washington Square Press.

G. P. Driver, *Canaanite Myths and Legends*. New York, Doubleday.

John Gray, *The Canaanites*. New York, Thames and Hudson, 1964.

J. G. Frazer, *The Golden Bough*, Part IV, New York, St. Martin's Press.

Mircea Eliade, *From the Primitives to Zen*. New York, Harper, 1966.

James B. Pritchard, ed., *The Ancient Near East: An Anthology of Texts and Pictures*. Princeton, N.J.; Princeton University Press, 1958.

E. A. Speiser, *Ancient Near East Texts*. Princeton, N.J.; Princeton University Press, 1950.

THEOLOGY:

A. Hulsbosch, O.S.A., *God in Creation and Evolution*. New York, Sheed and Ward, 1965.

Michael Schmaus, *Dogma,* Vol. II, *God and Creation*. New York, Sheed and Ward, 1969.

Karl Rahner, *Theological Investigations*, Vol. I. Baltimore, Helicon, 1961.

Herbert Haag, *Is Original Sin in Scripture?* New York, Sheed and Ward, 1969.

Karl Rahner, *Hominization*. New York, Herder and Herder.

Jean Daniélou, *Origen*. New York, Sheed and Ward.

Hans Urs von Balthasar, *A Theological Anthropology*. New York, Sheed and Ward, 1967.

SCIENCE:

Lancelot Pereira, ed., *Origins*. Poona, Pontifical Athenaeum, 1964 (an admirable study of Genesis in the light of modern science).

Charles Hauret, *Beginnings: Genesis and Modern Science*. Dubuque, Priory Press, 1953.

J. Lidyard Stebbins, *The Process of Organic Evolution*. New York, Prentice-Hall, 1966.

George and Muriel Beadle, *The Language of Life: An Introduction to Genetics*. New York, Doubleday, 1966.

Theodore Dobzhansky, *Mankind Evolving*. New Haven, Yale University Press, 1962.

Lionel S. Penrose, *An Outline of Human Genetics*. New York, John Wiley and Sons, Inc., 1963.

Harry Eldon Sutton, *An Introduction to Human Genetics*. New York, Holt, Rhinehart and Winston, 1965.

Sol Tax and Charles Callender, eds., *Evolution after Darwin*; Vol. III of "Issues in Evolution: The University of Chicago Centennial Discussion." Chicago, University of Chicago Press, 1960.

Sir Alister Hardy, *The Living Stream*, New York, Harper, 1963.

G. G. Simpson, *The Major Features of Evolution*. New York, Columbia University Press.

John W. Klotz, *Genes, Genesis and Evolution*. St. Louis, Mo.; Concordia, 1955.

Index

179